How to Prepare for the Coming Depression

A Workbook for Managing Your Money and Your Life During Economic Hard Times

By Mark Friedman
With Jack Miller

HOW TO PREPARE FOR THE COMING DEPRESSION
A Workbook for Managing Your Money and Your Life During Economic
Hard Times
by Mark Friedman with Jack Miller

Illustrations and book design by Michael B. McClure

Acknowledgments:
The author thanks Mary Friedman, Prahlad, Christine and Leila Karim,
Vimala and Michael McClure, Robin and Tom Arie-Donch, Kristie
Schellie, Bill Dorf, Robert Kaplan, Richard Friedman, Darlene Pearlstein,
Gail and Chuck Angell, Carol and Dan Sheehy, and P.R. Sarkar for their
love and support throughout this project.

Published by NUCLEUS Publications, Rte. 2, Box 49, Willow Springs, MO
65793. Send for free catalog.

First printing 1989

Library of Congress Cataloging in Publication Data

Friedman, Mark, 1951—
    How to Prepare for the Coming Depression: a Workbook for Manag-
ing Your Money and Your Life During Economic Hard Times by Mark
Friedman.
        p.   cm.
    Includes index.
    ISBN 0-94934-03-3 : $11.95
    1. Finance, Personal — United States.   2. Investments — United
States. 3. Business cycles — United States.   I. Title.
HG179.F734   1989
332.024'02—dc20   89-8668
                                                          CIP

Printed in the United States of America

To the Strength and Love
within us all

Foreword

How to Prepare for the Coming Depression is a comprehensive look at what you can do to get ready for the depression that grows nearer every day. Worldwide economic conditions continue much as I predicted in *The Great Depression of 1990* and *Surviving the Great Depression of 1990*. Little time remains before the onset of the next great crash and subsequent depression. Thus I urge you to read Mr. Friedman's book and develop a practical plan for preparation using the helpful guidelines he provides.

Mr. Friedman is clearly an excellent communicator who is able to capsulize economic concepts in a direct and well organized manner. The financial and career advice contained in this book is sound. He offers a conservative investment approach.

Protecting your current assets is much wiser than attempting to increase your assets with risky speculative ventures. As I point out in *Surviving the Great Depression of 1990*, the bubble of speculation is stretching thinner and will no doubt burst in the near future. The fallout from this explosion will make the "meltdown" of October, 1987 seem mild.

Mr. Friedman is particularly profound in his explanation of changes in behavior and attitudes that will best prepare you for the depression. The integration of financial, career, lifestyle, family, spiritual, and community preparation that he proposes is invaluable. Using even a small part of the charts and planning tools in this book will put you well ahead of those whose heads are still in the sand, unaware of the storm that is about to descend.

Drawing upon his extensive background in the human services, Mr. Friedman reminds the reader of the self-defeating nature of selfishness. With compassion and grace he challenges us to go beyond our own anxiety over the depression and reach out to others with the loving hand of service. Through thinking not only of ourselves, but also our families, our communities and our world, we can lessen the suffering the depression may bring. Together we can bear burdens that are individually insurmountable.

How to Prepare for the Coming Depression is a book of hope — hope in the resiliency and adaptability of human beings, and hope for our future. The reordering of priorities Mr. Friedman suggests is both beneficial and vitally necessary if we are all to survive the challenges and struggles that loom. I salute Mr. Friedman for the perspective and wisdom he brings to this book. I trust you will find it as helpful and meaningful as I do.

— Dr. Ravi Batra

Table of Contents

Chapter
1
A Chance to Change

The coming economic depression is unavoidable. An $8 trillion debt in the United States, the $990 billion in the third world, the precarious world banking system, the extreme concentration of wealth (1% of the population owns 36% of the wealth), and a dramatic convergence of economic cycles all point to economic disaster. But the reality of a depression need not be cause for despair. Rather, it can be the catalyst for growth — an opportunity to make positive changes in our lives and our world.

In the time remaining before the depression, you have the opportunity to thoroughly examine yourself, your family, and your community. The changes you make as a result can put you in the best possible position to not only survive the depression, but to triumph. Transforming your finances, your lifestyle, and your outlook is not an easy process, but one that is of paramount importance if you wish to emerge unscathed from the societal whirlwind that looms. None of us will emerge unchanged, but those who make the effort to prepare will be able to benefit from the transformation.

The traditional concept of benefit is unfortunately most often tied to personal financial gain. Of course, we are responsible for our families and must ensure that our loved ones are able to survive. However, the future of our planet depends upon our ability to grow from narrow self-interest to an understanding of the interconnectedness of all living beings. Thinking only of ourselves as we prepare for and live through a major depression may improve our material lot in life, but it will make our world a much worse place in which to live. The divisiveness born of greed and selfishness will only multiply everyone's difficulties and greatly increase the risk of planetary, environmental, and nuclear disaster.

Thinking of "me first" may be necessary in a society that provides few vehicles for guaranteeing the minimum necessities for all. We cannot rely on others to provide our food, clothing, shelter, and medical care. This book is about how to provide strength and security for your family and begin to reach out to your neighbors and community to make a positive difference. But a "me *only*" mentality fosters an orgy of accumulation that continues well after a person's needs are met. If the material resources of our planet were unlimited, this orgy would be unfortunate only for those who are fattening their wallets and diminishing their spirits, because there would be enough to satisfy the needs of all. However, our resources are limited. There is a direct connection between over-accumulation by individuals, corporations, and nations and ecological disaster and human suffering at home and abroad.

How to Prepare for the Coming Depression is not a philosophical treatise on economics, politics, or investments. It is a practical resource book that provides information to aid you in making good decisions. Like any resource book, some of the information may be more helpful to you, and some less so. You do not have to swallow this book whole. Please feel free to choose what you can use and reject that which is not relevant to your situation.

Few of us want to force our families into a survival lifestyle, especially when we may not be convinced it is absolutely necessary. However, the risk in waiting until after the depression has begun is that your economic, emotional, and spiritual resources may be stretched very thin at a time when you most need them. By planning and acting now, you can stay ahead of potentially devastating changes and successfully moderate how they affect you. If you shy away from this effort now, you are much more likely to be a victim of forces over which you have no control.

All areas of life are interdependent, and your preparation will be most effective if you approach it in a comprehensive manner. Your finances affect your emotions and your family. Your community affects your environment and thus your resources. Your health and emotional well being affect your ability to provide for your family and their potential for happiness in the midst of struggle.

The challenges you face in preparing for the depression may seem overwhelming, but try not to throw up your hands and decide to do nothing. Fearing that the depression is inexorably marching to your door and taking no positive action to get ready may leave you feeling worse than people who are unaware of what is coming. A more beneficial response is to start in a small way to make practical changes and gradually integrate more and more of these suggestions into your life. Depending on when the depression comes, you may be able to implement many of your desired preparations in this gradual and manageable way. For those of you reading this after the depression has begun, focus on the areas where your family will realize the most immediate positive benefit.

It is vital to prioritize those changes which are most important and practical for you. You obviously can't do it all, so select the areas you care about the most and get started. Determine which areas you will address later. Make copies of some of the charts and questionnaires and periodically review them to see how you are progressing. Putting it in writing is a valuable tool for helping you to change.

Try to build upon successes by making attainable changes your top priorities. If you decide that your first priority is to save 50% of your income and this proves impossible, you will be discouraged from making any changes. As pointed out in the chapter on the importance of family, be sure to include your children in the whole process whenever possible. The decisions and changes you make will dramatically affect their lives, and they will participate much more willingly and with greater understanding if they feel their voices are heard.

The opportunities that will come out of preparation include the joy and satisfaction that come from taking control of our lives and fostering positive values and lifestyles. Decreasing our reliance on material things and nurturing the love within each one of us and our families will reap benefits that enrich us beyond measure. Reaching out to our community and those in need ennobles our lives and provides the foundation for healing our planet. With a positive transformation of our way of living, we can emerge from the coming hard times stronger, healthier, and better able to live in harmony with ourselves and all living beings.

Chapter

2

Why Another Depression is Inevitable

Investors of the 1920's were convinced they had entered a new era of ever-increasing stock prices and economic prosperity. The crash of 1929 and the subsequent Depression shattered this conviction. Since the 1930's, every generation has comforted itself with the illusion of increased wisdom and safeguards against the advent of another depression. Unfortunately, the evidence shows that not only is the economy not depression proof, but it is teetering on a precipice.

The 508 point (22.6%) one-day drop in the Dow Jones Industrial Average on October 19, 1987 fueled fears that history will repeat and the economy will plunge into another Great Depression with widespread bankruptcies, bank closures, and unemployment. Over half of the 105 top corporate executives surveyed by the University of Wisconsin felt there was a "high probability" there would be a major depression in the next ten years.[1] This survey was taken before "Meltdown Monday." Five main areas of crisis point to a depression:

1. Debt and deficit
2. Bank instability
3. Stock market speculation
4. Concentration of wealth
5. Economic cycles

Each of these factors alone may or may not trigger a depression but the conjunction of all five in the later part of the 1980's leads to only one conclusion: there is no way to avoid a major depression.

DEBT AND DEFICIT

Overall debt in the United States

In the past two years, the United States surpassed Brazil, Mexico and Argentina to become the largest debtor nation in the world. The total government, corporate, and individual debt has passed $8,000,000,000,000 (eight trillion dollars), twice the gross national product. The government's share of this debt is $2.3 trillion. Tied for second place in the debt parade are American corporations and home mortgages with $1.5 trillion each, followed by $500 billion in installment credit.[2] The annual budget deficit which adds to the national debt climbed to over $200 billion under President Reagan's administration.

These figures indicate that, as a nation, we have mortgaged our future. Much of this debt is owed to foreign banks and investors who, in essence, control the financial future of the United States. Sooner or later these debts come due. Already 14% of the national budget (14 cents of every dollar spent) goes to service existing debt; that figure grows every year through the medium of compound interest.[3]

Third World debt

The debt owed by less developed countries to the International Monetary Fund (IMF), the World Bank, and U.S. and European banks has reached gigantic proportions (over $990 billion) and forced some of the largest U.S. banks to begin to write off bad loans. About half of this $990 billion is owed to commercial banks.

The IMF (a United Nations sponsored loan fund) stands ready as the lender of last resort for the less developed countries. These countries borrow money to make payments on their previous loans, and the merry-go-round goes blithely on.   Loan "re-structuring" forces debtor governments to impose severe austerity measures, increasing the suffering of millions of people. Rising political and social unrest in poor countries could finally end the game and send the world monetary system crashing down — leading to depression in the industrial nations. However, it is important to realize that for many countries in the developing world, depression has been a daily reality for decades. The starvation and misery in countries like Mexico, Haiti, Sudan, Brazil, India, and Mozambique is the dark underside of the glittering illusion of economic health under the current system.

U.S. trade deficit

The U.S. annual trade deficit is the measure of the amount of goods imported versus the amount exported. It grew from zero in 1975 to $176 billion in 1987. Lower labor costs abroad, the strong dollar, and a perceived lesser quality in many American products have all contributed to this dramatic change. Japan and western Europe have been the major beneficiaries. The result is a flood of dollars flowing overseas. To compound the problem, the very money that American consumers use to buy Japanese and German imports is borrowed by the U.S. government to finance the annual deficit and national debt. Paul Volcker, former head of the Federal Reserve Board, testified at a congressional hearing, "We don't generate enough savings at home to finance the deficit. We are relying on capital inflow from foreign investors to finance our deficit. In a very real sense, we cannot afford to correct the trade deficit."

Continuing trade deficits force the U.S. economy to depend on foreign investors who are increasingly nervous about locking up their trade surpluses in U.S. dollars and U.S. Treasury securities. John Kenneth Galbraith says, "The danger is that we have accumulated under the Reagan Administration such enormous overseas obligations that these could, if liquidated, create a very, very nasty run on the dollar and also a nasty collapse of the stock market."[4]

Corporate debt

Corporations have steadily increased their debt by $150 billion a year throughout the 1980's. In the 1970's about one quarter of corporate cash flow went to service debt. Now over half of corporate income goes for interest payments.[5] Through imaginative vehicles such as junk bonds and leveraged buyouts, corporations have increased their debt to equity ratios for non-financial corporations from 73.7% in 1983 to 87.6% in 1985. Another stock market crash and/or a recession could substantially increase these ratios to a level where dominoing defaults could become commonplace. Already the number of corporations with the highest credit rating (AAA) has decreased by 50% in the last ten years.

Corporations are often forced to increase their debt to prevent hostile takeovers. Corporate raiders pick off cash rich companies as juicy plums. The raider can use the company's own cash to mount its campaign. Many companies have diverted countless resources from research, development, and production in order to fight unfriendly raiders. Objects of takeover bids who fight often take on new mountains of debt to create a war chest. When Corning was raided, they had to lay off 500 research people to fight the takeover.

The *Quick Ratio* is a measure of a company's ability to withstand short term losses and financial shocks. It is determined by taking the amount of cash and liquid assets such as Treasury bills and dividing by debt obligations that are due within a year. The lower the Quick Ratio, the shakier the company. For manufacturing companies, this figure has steadily declined from 1.07 in the late 40's to 0.15 in the early 80's.[6]

Consumer debt

The American Dream is of a constantly improving quality of life. As a nation we finance this dream by going into debt. Consumer debt tripled in the last ten years while average real income showed no increase.[7] Most consumer debt is financed with credit cards and home equity loans. Outstanding credit card debt reached $150 billion by the end of 1987. Credit card delinquencies reached 3%.[8] Estimates of the amount of after tax income Americans spend on credit obligations range from 20% to 33%. Personal bankruptcies rose 35% in 1986, a strong indication that individuals are finding it increasingly difficult to cope with these debts. These bankruptcies occurred during a time of relative economic prosperity. During economic downturns when the ranks of the unemployed burgeon, the rate of bankruptcies and fore-closures will explode.

The connection between debt and depression

Common sense, which has become rare in our economy, tells us that sooner or later the spiraling debt will stop. Credit indicates trust and the belief that the debtor will repay the obligations incurred when they come due; the shattering of that trust brings consequences: Consumers, accounting for 66% of the GNP, no longer have the money to maintain the level of consumption necessary to drive the economy.[9] Corporations lack the capital not only to expand but also to maintain the same levels of production and employment. The government is unable to obtain the money it needs to operate, and deficits increase as tax revenues decrease. No one is willing to loan the money needed to finance the deficit. The result is depression. This collapse of credit has happened in all previous depressions, and there has never been anything like the current mind-boggling debt in the United States.

Based upon his studies of the work of Russian economist Nicholai Kondratieff, Douglas Kirkland calculates the current ratio of debt to actual currency (in the form of dollars and gold) in the United States to be thirty to one. This is unprecedented. In 1928 the ratio was fifteen to one. Kirkland predicts that, through such vehicles as options and futures contracts, the ratio could reach as much as forty to one before a necessary crash and deflation corrects the imbalance through massive bankruptcy and default. In previous depressions the ratio was restored to a safe level of ten to one.[10]

BANK INSTABILITY

Banks and Third World debt

Debt accumulation jeopardizes the world financial and banking system. The instability of major banks is primarily manifested in over $400 billion in loans to developing countries, notably Mexico, Brazil, and Argentina. In 1982 Mexico declared itself unable to continue making interest payments on its $85 billion in loans. Nine major U.S. banks discovered that their combined loans to Latin American countries were equivalent to 75% more than their combined capital.[11] They turned to the government, and Federal Reserve Chairman Paul Volcker arranged for billions in public funds to help Mexico pay interest on its loans.

Why did the government bail out the megabanks which had dug their own graves by questionable banking practices? They had no choice. The future of the international monetary system was hanging on the edge. In recent years debtor nations have realized the power they hold in the threat of default. In 1985, Peru announced it would pay its creditors only 10% of its earnings from exports. In 1986, Brazil and Venezuela unilaterally announced that they would set their own payment schedules and not wait for IMF imposed austerity programs. The tenuousness of international banking is such that the lenders have virtually no leverage. If only one major debtor nation repudiates its loans, a domino effect will cause massive bank failures.

International development projects encourage Third World countries to take on huge loans to build Western style economies and cash crop agriculture. The resulting programs force people off their land and lead to widespread migration to cities in search of work. It also forces these countries to import food they previously grew. Growing hunger and disenfranchisement lead to social unrest and falling productivity. Debt rises. Suddenly the so-called developing country finds itself with a hungry populace, impossible loan burdens, and a need for periodic payment rescheduling.

This process demonstrates that money loaned to developing countries does not help the poor and suffering people of the debtor nations. Unfortunately, huge percentages of the money loaned winds up in the pockets of rulers, dictators, and favored businessmen such as Ferdinand Marcos and Jean-Claude "Baby Doc" Duvalier. It is estimated that 40% of Mexico's borrowed money, 60% of Argentina's, and all of Venezuela's money leaked into private hands and wound up right back at the big banks in the form of private deposits.[12]

These bad loans rebound back onto U.S. and other Western banks. As the result of sovereign debt from less developed countries, major banks such as Bank America, Chase, Citicorp, Chemical, and Manufacturers Hanover all have loan-to-capital ratios that are well over 100%.[13] If and when countries repudiate their debts, major American banks will fail without a massive infusion of government capital. But there is a limit to what the government will be able to do without straining the Federal Reserve to the breaking point. Printing money to cover bad debts leads to runaway inflation. Asking the taxpayers to foot the bill spirals deficits out of control. If no other bank steps forward to take over insolvent banks, the Federal Deposit Insurance Corporation must, and the bank is essentially nationalized at taxpayer expense. There is already a contingency plan for wholesale nationalization of banks.[14]

Banks and domestic debt

The rest of the story is not much rosier. Due to foreclosures and falling real estate prices in much of the U.S., as well as questionable energy and agricultural loans, savings and loans and commercial banks are failing at a rate not seen since the 1930's. 138 banks failed in 1986; 208 failed in 1987 . The $18 billion in the FDIC fund cannot absorb many more bank failures. In mid-1985, a study found that over half of commercial banks' $51 billion in loans to farmers were "dangerously delinquent." Twenty six percent of all farm banks were classified as being in trouble.[15]

The Federal Savings and Loan Insurance Corporation (FSLIC) is in even worse shape. Over 800 savings and loans are operating at a loss, and 250 have a negative net worth, with an annual loss of almost $10 billion.[16] The latest administration plan to bail out insolvent Savings and Loans will only begin to address the problem. A nationwide run on Savings and Loans would find many depositors out of luck.

The connection between failing banks and depression

The stock market crash of 1929 contributed to the economic collapse and the Depression of the 1930's, but it was the chaos of international banking that really caused the worst problems. People's belief in the security of their money in banks is essential to their sense of economic well being. When banks fail, panic sets in, and unchecked panic leads to total economic collapse. Total economic collapse leads to depression and years before recovery. Economist Lester Thurow states, "Stock markets don't bring economies down. Collapsing banks bring economies down."[17]

STOCK MARKET SPECULATION

Stock markets may not bring economies down by themselves, but throughout history they have provided the trigger to many collapses. In the past eighty years, stock price drops of 10% or more were associated with seventeen of eighteen recessions.[18] The five year bull market on Wall Street brought the Dow Jones Industrial Average to new heights, greatly increasing the paper wealth of many investors. As the crash of October 19, 1987 showed, this paper wealth can disappear quickly.

A whole class of people has been created who achieve wealth without producing products or services. Apart from the moral question of whether wealth without work is desirable, the economic consequence is that less money is invested in creating jobs and expanding technology and industry. When investors find they can make more money by speculating than by investing in long term production, the economy suffers.

The feeding frenzy in financial markets increases volatility, which hampers steady economic growth. At the start of the bull market in August, 1982, investors looked for stocks based on their worth as measured by corporate profits and dividends. In its later stages, the bull market is driven by pure speculation. In Tokyo, the frenzy has been even more pronounced, as shares have traded at triple the price to earnings ratio of New York stocks.[19]

The purchase of stock on slim margins (percentage of stock purchase price paid as down payments) was viewed as one of major contributing factors to the 1929 crash. As stock prices turned lower, investors were faced with dreaded margin calls, forcing them to ante up more cash or liquidate their holdings. This greatly accelerated the negative market momentum. Today, stock margin requirements are 50%, and fewer investors buy their stock on margin. However, commodities futures contracts require as little as 3% to 5% margins. Widespread corporate takeovers and mergers financed by junk bonds and bank funded leveraged buyouts have created a new form of over-leveraging. When the market turns down, many of these bonds will become worthless. Banks that fund takeovers will be left holding the bag on debt that is not supportable by corporate equity or earnings.

In 1929 only 8% of individuals owned stocks. Now, through profit sharing, insurance companies, mutual funds, pension and union funds, it is estimated that 85% of the population participates in the stock market. An escalating and prolonged market crash will speed a plunge as individuals find their pension and insurance nest eggs severely diminished. In response to this, it is likely they will decrease spending, causing lower demand and production.

Speculative manias fuel themselves and stretch a bubble to extremely tenuous limits before bursting. The result is at best, economic recession, and at worst, depression. The Wall Street debacle of October, 1987 may be just a taste of what we are likely to see in the coming years.

CONCENTRATION OF WEALTH

John Kenneth Galbraith cites unequal distribution of income as one of the main reasons for the Great Crash of 1929 and the subsequent Depression.[20] Now, the wealthiest 10% of U.S. families hold 68% of the nation's assets.[21] Current figures show that 1% of the population owns 36% of the U.S. assets. This is the highest concentration of wealth since 1929, when 1% of the population owned 37% of U.S. assets. Besides the obvious inequity of such a concentration of wealth, the overall economic consequences are grave.

The wealthy, because of their limited numbers, can only spend a limited amount on consumer goods. An upper level corporate executive's salary may exceed the total of 25 lower echelon employees, but his employees will spend more money — helping the economy. The late 1920's and recent years have seen less wealth going to expansion of plants and economic development and more money going to fuel financial speculation. The skyrocketing speculative bubble creates more paper wealth and further increases the concentration in the hands of speculators.

Supply-side economics, which Ronald Reagan heartily embraced, assumed that the massive tax cuts of 1981 would free up money for savings and investment. However, both savings and investment have decreased. Gross fixed investment as a percentage of the Gross National Product (GNP) has decreased from 17.6% in 1979 to 14.9% today. In Japan, investment is 28% of GNP, and in Germany it is about 20%.[22] Is it any wonder, then, that we are losing the trade war? The $6.7 trillion spent on defense in the last 30 years could have easily financed the rebuilding of every factory, bridge, and road in the United States.[23]

Wealth inequality further causes the poor and middle class to support their lifestyles through consumer borrowing. The explosion of consumer debt further damages the soundness of banks and the financial systems. A study by the Urban Institute found that the buying power of poor people decreased by 40% between 1981 and 1984. Yet debt-fueled spending increased. The Center for Budget and Policy Priorities reported in 1985 that the gap between the rich and the poor was greater than at any time since they started to collect data on income distribution in 1947.[24]

ECONOMIC CYCLES

From the economic forecasts of Nicholai Kondratieff in 1922 to the present prognostication of Robert Prechter and Ravi Batra, economists have been fascinated with the search for underlying order in seemingly random economic occurrences. Kondratieff predicted the depression of the 1930's, and for his success and unorthodox theories he was exiled by the Soviet regime to Siberia where he died. Prechter and Batra have been two of the most successful present day economic forecasters, judging by their track records. Batra's record of predictions regarding interest rates, conflict in the Middle East, inflation, and the stock market boom is unmatched. Prechter has been considered the top stock market forecaster for several years. His influence with investors is such that many observers credited his advice as a contributing factor to the huge market losses from October 15 through the 20th of 1987.

Kondratieff studied economic history using statistics dating back to 1789. He believed that the long-term business cycle lasts from forty-five to sixty years and is characterized by upswing, crisis, and depression. He did not give precise lengths to these periods, but he pointed out how to recognize the trends that signal which cycle the economy is in. According to Kondratieff's followers, the period preceding a depression is one of plateau and is characterized by depressed agriculture, slow economic growth, low inflation, relatively high unemployment, escalating

Economic Parallels Between the 1920's and 1980's

	1920's	1980's
Stock Market	Boom—prices doubled from 1925 to 1929	Boom—prices more than tripled from 1982 to 1987
Inflation	High at beginning of decade, turning low in 1922	High at beginning of decade, turning low in 1982
Taxes	Huge tax cut in 1921	Huge tax cut in 1981
Employment	High unemployment at start of decade, declining sharply in 1923	High unemployment at start of decade, declining sharply in 1983
Energy Prices	Sharp decline in mid decade	Sharp decline in mid decade
Interest Rates	High at beginning of decade, declining sharply in 1922	High at beginning of decade, declining sharply in 1982
Labor	Union membership declines by 28% from 1920 to 1930, minimum wage increases	Union membership declines by 15.4% by mid decade, minimum wage increases
Debt	Soars to unprecedented levels fueling consumer spending, stock market boom, and mergers	Soars to unprecedented levels fueling consumer spending, mergers, takeovers, and government deficits
New Investment Vehicles	Investment trusts and utility pyramids explode	Junk bonds, leveraged buyouts and stock index futures explode
Agriculture	Depressed throughout decade; farm foreclosures increase; commodities prices decline	Depressed throughout decade; farm foreclosures increase; commodities prices decline
Banks	Bank failures rise sharply starting in mid decade; banks offer checking with interest for the first time in 1922; banks speculate heavily in the stock market	Bank failures rise sharply starting in mid decade; banks offer checking with interest in 1982 for the first time since the 1930's; banks try to lift restrictions on stock investing imposed in 1933
Concentration of Wealth	Grows throughout decade to 1% of population owning 37% of wealth at time of crash in 1929	Grows throught decade to 1% of population owning 36% of wealth in late 1987
Economic Growth	Recession to start decade, then steady growth	Recession to start decade, then steady growth

financial markets, and conservatism. In other words, this plateau or "downwave," as Kondratieff called it, is happening right now, and a depression is imminent.

Robert Prechter bases his work on the Eliott wave theory first introduced by R.N. Eliott in the 1930's. According to Prechter, "We are approaching the end of a 200-year grand supercycle, and it is clearly unfolding the classic five-wave pattern described by R.N. Elliot." The 200-year grand supercycle began in 1789 and is scheduled to end in 1989 with a cataclysmic crash worse than 1929, according to Prechter.

Ravi Batra, the author of *The Great Depression of 1990,* cites a pattern of thirty-year and sixty-year cycles of inflation, money growth, and government regulation which he correlates with recession and depression.[25] By his calculations, the end of 1989 will bring the beginning of a worldwide economic depression that will dwarf the Depression of the 1930's. His conclusion is that if, at the thirty-year mark there is no economic downturn, then at the sixty-year mark the downturn will be severe. 1930 saw the start of the Great Depression, and 1960 saw no recession or depression. Batra expects the 1990's to bring the worst depression in history.

In addition to the cyclical observations of Kondratieff, Prechter, and Batra, many people have noted the uncanny resemblance of the decade of the 1980's to the decade of the 1920's. Some of the economic parallels are noted in the chart on the preceding page.

There is a growing conviction among many economists and observers that the primary question is no longer if there will be a depression, but when. The time bomb is ticking. As Galbraith observed in *The Great Crash,* "Long run salvation by men of business has never been highly regarded if it means disturbance of orderly life and convenience in the present." Not only businessmen, but politicians and the general public show a reluctance to confront the crisis head on. Rather than making sacrifices now, we prefer to forestall disaster as long as possible. It is much easier to avoid difficult decisions and pretend it can't happen again.

In September of 1928, Andrew W. Mellon, Secretary of the Treasury, said, "There is no cause for worry. The high tide of prosperity will continue." President Calvin Coolidge addressed Congress on December 4, 1928, stating, "No Congress of the United States ever assembled, on surveying the state of the Union, has met with a more pleasing prospect than that which appears at this time." One would think the same ageless speech writers are writing the script for our current leaders. It will take real leadership and a willingness to reorder our priorities to stop the depression from coming. So far, there is nothing to indicate that this will happen.

Endnotes

1. Stephen Koepp, *Time*, October 5, 1987.
2. Lawrence Malkin, *The National Debt* (New York: Henry Holt, 1987), p. 5.
3. Executive Office of the President, *The United States Budget in Brief, Fiscal Year 1988* (January 5, 1987).
4. Koepp, p. 46.
5. Malkin, p. 54.
6. Alfred L. Malabre, Jr., *Beyond Our Means,* (New York: Random House, 1987), p. 30.
7. Malkin, p. 49.
8. *Rocky Mountain News,* August 30, 1987, p. 72.
9. *Business Week,* November 16, 1987, p. 165.
10. *The Economist,* April 18, 1987, p. 73.
11. Malkin, p. 77.
12. Malkin, p. 84.
13. Jack Anderson and Michael Binstein, *Parade Magazine,* September 20, 1987, p. 15.
21. L.J. Davis, *Harper's Magazine,* May, 1987.
22. Karen Pennar, *Business Week,* November 16, 1987, p. 166.
23. According to Seymour Melman, *Business Week,* November 16, 1987, p. 166.
24. Gregory Bergman, *Monthly Review,* October, 1986, p. 30.
25. Ravi Batra, *The Great Depression of 1990,* (New York: Simon and Schuster, 1987).

Chapter
3
Experiencing the Depression

The specter of another depression leads us back to previous depressions to get an idea of what we can expect. Historian Barbara Tuchman said, "History is a great joker always likely to take an unexpected turn for which no one has planned. Its lessons cannot tell us what will happen next, but only how people tend to react."[1] A generation of economists and statisticians found work trying to make economic sense out of the Depression and to quantify its effects. The statistics of depressions can be useful indicators of the scope of the problem, but they fail to truly express the human suffering that has made the very word "depression" strike fear and trembling into the hearts of millions. Understanding depressions more clearly can help diminish our fears. Panic can be a tremendous motivator, but it also carries a cloud of unreason that stifles creative and positive solutions to the underlying problem. While a reasonable concern will help mobilize your efforts to prepare for and respond to a depression, fear will contribute little to your endeavors.

There have been several depressions since the Revolutionary War. Most observers agree that the 1840's, 1870's, and 1930's all brought full fledged depressions characterized by economic decline and high unemployment. The 1890's also saw a pervasive economic downturn that probably deserves to be classified as a depression. All U.S. depressions have taken remarkably similar courses. Because the Great Depression of the 1930's was the deepest and most recent, a history of its development presents a good general picture of the course of a depression.

THE GREAT DEPRESSION OF THE 1930'S

The Great Depression began in the early summer of 1929 as consumption and factory orders declined precipitously. The full impact of how this affected the economy did not make itself known for a while. Until "Black Tuesday," October 29, 1929, a mood of unmitigated optimism permeated Wall Street and the country. There were few to disagree with President Calvin Coolidge when he delivered the following message to Congress in December of 1928:

"The great wealth created by our enterprise and industry, and saved by our economy, has had the widest distribution among our own people, and has gone out in a steady stream to serve the charity and the business of the world. The requirements of existence have passed beyond the standard of necessity into the region of luxury . . . The country can regard the present with satisfaction and anticipate the future with optimism."[2]

The optimism of Coolidge was dashed, millions of investors were stunned, and the country as a whole was shattered by the 40% decline of stock market prices from September to November, 1929. What began as a recession in the summer rapidly turned into an all-out economic collapse that spread to every corner of the globe by mid-1930. Unemployment, which had been at a minimal level of 4%, soared to 21% in 1930, and reached 32% in 1932 — leaving 15 million people jobless at the depth of the Depression. The jobless rate remained well above 10% throughout the decade.

The Gross National Product (GNP) plummeted by 30% from 1929 to 1933 and did not reach 1929 levels until a halting recovery of the economy in 1936. From 1929 to 1933, personal consumption of durable goods fell by 50%, new construction by 80%, and producers' durable equipment by 67%.

Nondurable goods decline much less in any economic downturn. People need food, water, clothing, and heat to survive. As long as they are breathing, they will spend every available dime to get what their families need for basic sustenance. From 1929 to 1933, consumable goods and services declined 15%. The recovery of 1936 stalled, and another recession in 1937 again depressed the GNP. It took until 1941, as the country and world geared up for global conflict, for full economic recovery.

Every depression in the U.S. has been marked by deflation, since money is more scarce than goods and services. Wholesale prices dropped by one third between 1929 and 1932 and remained in decline throughout the decade. In 1941, they were still almost 10% less than they had been in 1929. Consumer prices fell by one fourth between 1929 and 1933 and also remained depressed throughout the decade. By 1941, consumer prices were still 14.5% less than 1929 levels. Widespread defaults on loans and loss of property through tax delinquencies left a tremendous glut of farms, homes, and assets of all kinds that further depressed prices. Other aspects of the Depression included widespread closures of banks (nearly 8,000 out of a total of 24,000) and a sharp decline in industrial output and corporate profits. The only industry that expanded in the Depression was the government! Decreases in revenue ranged from 30% in communications and public utilities to 65% in manufacturing, 68% in mining, and a staggering 80% in contract construction.[3] The only types of corporations to make profits during the Depression were those dealing in nondurable goods, including utilities, food manufacturers, and producers of petroleum, gas, and chemicals. Large corporations fared better because they were more able to service their debts. Thousands of smaller companies either went bankrupt or were swallowed up by expanding corporate giants.

UNEMPLOYMENT AND ITS EFFECTS

Pervasive unemployment is the most dramatic result of depressions. The most lasting image of the 1930's is of millions of jobless people in misery. Cabell Phillips, commenting on that time, wrote, "Mass unemployment is both a statistic and an empty feeling in the stomach. To fully comprehend it, you have to both see the figures and feel the emptiness."[4]

At the depth of the Great Depression in 1932, an estimated 40 million people were left with no regular source of income. An unemployed miner wrote to President Roosevelt, "We have been eating wild greens, such as Polk Salad, Violet tops, wild onions, forget-me-not, wild lettuce and such weeds as cows eat as a cow won't eat poison weeds." An investigator found some children in Kentucky so hungry that they were chewing on their hands.[5] Mass starvation was not apparent, but mass malnourishment and hunger were obvious: from thousands huddling in bread lines to children crying themselves to sleep with hunger pains. Fights broke out at some trash heaps, where leftover refuse represented the basic food source for thousands of people.

Illness in families of the jobless was 66% greater than that among families with a full-time worker. Lack of nourishing food led to greater disease and lower life expectancy for many. Walter de la Mare's poem *The Slum Child* spoke of the plight of many.

In leafless Summer's stench and noise
I'd sit and play
With other as lean-faced girls and boys
And sticks and stones for toys.
Then up the noisome stairs I'd creep
For food and rest
Or empty bellied, lie and weep
My silly woes to sleep.
What evil and filth and poverty
In childhood harboured me.[6]

The suffering of children is the most heart-wrenching result of a depression. Malnourished children with swollen bellies dressed in tattered hand-me-downs were a common sight in most large cities. Many teachers tell of poor school attendance because many pupils had no shoes and were too ashamed to come to school.

Stages of unemployment

The length of unemployment varied greatly, with some workers out of work for six months, others as long as ten years. The estimated average time out of work for the jobless approached two years. The long-term unemployed went through several stages, according to John Garraty, a chronicler of the Depression. At first they felt it was only temporary, and they would cut back on "luxuries." Then they would frantically search for employment with a fierce determination, cutting out all unnecessary expenditures, and buying on credit whenever possible. They tended to blame being out of work on bad luck. During the next stage, the jobless gave up even looking for work and no longer worried about keeping up appearances. A withdrawal from social interaction took place. They stopped looking ahead or making plans. During the last stage, resignation set in, and a permanent adjustment was made when they lost hope of ever finding jobs. People in this stage spent money when they had it, and accepted relief and charity when available.[7]

Paul Lazarfield made extensive studies of the town of Marienthal, Austria where practically the whole village was unemployed. He observed four basic types of adjustment: The "unbroken" continued to stay relatively optimistic and look for work and make some plans. Then came the "resigned," by far the largest group (over half the people studied), who had no prospects or expectations for the future. The third category, "the despairing," descended into gloom and undirected rage. This group was most likely to turn to alcohol and domestic violence. The last group were deemed the "apathetic," the poorest of the poor, who had given up entirely.[8]

Unemployment effect on individuals

Some of the best descriptions of the effect of prolonged unemployment were made by novelists George Orwell, John Dos Passos, Nathanel West and Theodore Dreiser and poets such as Stephen Spender. The following poem by Spender described a common scene of the unemployed:

> *Moving through the silent crowd*
> *Who stand behind dull cigarettes*
> *These men who idle in the road,*
> *I have the sense of falling light.*
> *They lounge at corners of the street*
> *And greet friends with a shrug of the shoulder*

And turn their empty pockets out,
The cynical gestures of the poor.
I'm haunted by these images,
I'm haunted by their emptiness.

In the English novel *Love on the Dole*, a character, referring to unemployment, says *"[it] got you slowly, with the slippered stealth of an unsuspected malignant disease. You fell into the habit of slouching, of putting your hands into your pockets and keeping them there; of glancing at people furtively, ashamed of your secret, until you fancied that everybody eyed you with suspicion."[9]*

One of the most devastating consequences of prolonged unemployment is the loss of self-esteem. For a man who was accustomed to being the breadwinner, it was humbling to be unable to provide for his family. Often decision making would shift to the woman of the family, and the children would lose respect for their out-of-work father. They didn't understand why Dad sat at home all day. Those families that were able to adjust positively could enjoy having the father home spending more time with the children and taking care of household chores.

The United States had a strong commitment to individualism and the work ethic. This made depressions especially hard for people to understand and accept. Many had been raised on the stories of Horatio Alger which glorified the belief that anyone who worked hard enough could raise him or herself up "by the bootstraps" and succeed in the great land of opportunity. Consequently, the most widespread reaction to unemployment was that it was the individual's own fault. Rather than blaming the Depression, big business, or the government, the unemployed generally felt it was some personal defect that prevented them from finding work. This reaction was a major reason why there was relatively little social unrest in the country. Apart from several protracted and violent labor strikes and the Veteran's Bonus March of 1932, the poor and jobless were remarkably docile.

President Herbert Hoover wrote, "Many persons left their jobs for the more profitable one of selling apples."[10] The notion that the unemployed were shiftless and lazy was routinely used as an argument against providing relief or government jobs, an argument which many studies refuted. Often the unemployed refused to accept assistance, when available, out of pride and self-reliance. Most people had centered their lives around full-time employment, and their most fervent wish was to obtain work and get back on their feet.

Social workers and the unemployed universally preferred subsidized employment to welfare — "the dole." Work was much more sustaining and life-affirming than being forced to accept handouts. A person's self-esteem is nurtured by working and making a meaningful contribution to society. The unemployed are generally unable to feel good about themselves.

THE SOCIAL IMPACT OF ECONOMIC COLLAPSE

Depressions and the unemployment they bring have far-reaching consequences for a whole society. Although many had no personal experience of suffering, life in a time of depression has an intensity that affects all but the most callous. Many people who still held jobs (68% of workers, even at the time of highest unemployment) found themselves materially better off due to falling prices, but some of their friends, relatives, and neighbors had to be affected.

The wealthy, with the exception of those who lost everything in the stock market slide, bank or business failures, generally suffered little. Indeed oral histories, such as *Hard Times* by Studs Terkel, include interviews with people who were unaware of the bread lines or that there were people without clothing and shelter. In an age without television, it is possible that wealthy people could live their lives blithely ignorant of the misery and suffering a few miles away from their doorsteps.

Working together

One positive aspect of depressions is the necessity for people to work together for mutual support. In the 1890's, self-help projects flourished, including community gardens, labor exchanges, cooperative stores, farmers' railroads, and intentional communities. During the 1930's, many cooperatives were started — often with the help of churches. When people realized they could not solve all their problems individually and that the government could not provide for all, they often turned to their friends and neighbors. Working together, people initiated many impressive self-help projects, some of which are still functioning today.

When people opened their hearts to help others, suffering was alleviated. Neighbors took in the families of their jobless friends; children helped bring in the money for their families' rent and food. Private charitable agencies fed millions; and some provided work to thousands. Community charity drives kept many families from starvation. When people's spirits were nourished by voluntary acts of kindness, communities grew closer together and everyone benefited. Depressions not only bring suffering, but also a tremendous opportunity to transcend feelings of alienation and self-interest and reach out to others in love and sacrifice. Inspiring stories of service give reason for optimism in the midst of misery.

Agriculture

Both of the last two depressions were preceded by depressions in agriculture. Farmers were plagued by low commodity prices, and thousands of farms were foreclosed. Once the Depression spread worldwide, the situation grew even worse for farmers, as commodities prices plunged even lower. In an effort to survive, farmers increased their output. More crops were produced, with the exception of cotton and tobacco. However, this increase in output did little to bring solvency to millions of farmers who struggled to meet their debt obligations.

The prices received by farmers for their crops declined by 57% from 1929 to 1933. The price of some of the most important farm prices declined even more. Corn fell from 80 cents a bushel to 32 cents a bushel; wheat from $1.04 a bushel to 38 cents a bushel; cotton from 17 cents a pound to 7 cents a pound; oranges from $3.59 a box to 88 cents a box,; and whole milk from $2.53 a gallon to $1.28.[11]

The discrepancy between the prices farmers paid for supplies and the payment they received at harvest exacerbated the problem. The parity ratio (a measure of what farmers pay to what they receive) fell from 92% in 1929 to 58% in 1932.[12] This led to a tremendous increase in the numbers of foreclosures and forced sales for tax delinquencies. Forced sales increased from 19.5 for every 1,000 farms to 41.7 in 1932.[13]

A poem written by agrarian Will Carlton in 1890 speaks to the plight of many farmers during depressions.

We worked through spring and winter, through summer and through fall
But the mortgage worked the hardest and steadiest of them all;
It worked on nights and Sundays, it worked each holiday;
It settled down among us and never went away . . .
And there came a dark day on us when the interest wasn't paid,
And there came a sharp foreclosure, and I kind o' lost my hold,
And grew weary and discouraged and the farm was cheaply sold.
The children left and scattered, when they hardly yet were grown;
. . . My wife she pined and perished, an' I found myself alone,
What she died of was a mystery, and the doctors never knew;
But I know she died of mortgage — just as well as I wanted to.[14]

The number of foreclosures would have increased even more dramatically if creditors saw anything to be gained by foreclosing. As the Depression wore on and banks and mortgage holders found themselves with many foreclosed properties, they realized it was better to tolerate delinquency than to be the landlord for thousands of farms that were difficult to rent and maintain. When the banks foreclosed and sold the property (if they could find a buyer), they had to take much less than the value of the mortgage and decrease their assets. Because most banks were already on extremely shaky ground, they could not afford to have to restate their assets and net worth. So although 45% of all mortgaged farms were delinquent on their loans, banks became increasingly reluctant to foreclose.

Even if farmers were able to stay on their farms, decreasing farm income left them with little or no cash. Fortunately, most of them were able to grow enough food to survive, but other household goods and necessities were extremely difficult to come by. Millions of farmers lived in abject poverty for much of the Depression.

Labor

Labor union membership declined at the start of the Depression and then gradually climbed. The 1920's, like the 1980's, was a time of decreased labor union membership. Total union membership declined from 5 million in 1920 to 3.4 million in 1929, and to less than 3 million in 1933. Relative to Europe, the U.S. had only a small percentage of union membership. Many people left the union when they lost their jobs because the unions could offer them little assistance. Almost all union members were in the building trades, mining, and a few skilled crafts. Few unskilled and mass production employees belonged to unions until after the Wagner Act in 1936, when John L. Lewis and the CIO (Congress of Industrial Organizations) began to organize them.

Traditional union leadership was conservative and did not support the unemployed. In 1932 when unemployment was over 10 million, the American Federation of Labor opposed government relief for the unemployed, because relief "instills in those cared for a sense of irresponsibility and dependence that is harmful to society." Also women and minorities were generally not permitted to join unions. Unions supported the policy adopted by most employers of "last hired, first fired," which discriminated against younger workers, women, and minorities.

Conditions became polarized between workers who maintained their jobs and those who were laid off. Generally, wages declined less than the cost of living, thus increasing purchasing power for those still at work. Conversely, the unemployed having no purchasing power, had no money to buy the less costly goods.

Housing

Depressions characteristically left many of the jobless with no place to live. Homeowners faced foreclosure, and renters faced eviction. Both foreclosures and evictions were especially prevalent during the first few years of the Depression. Once banks and landlords held countless vacant properties, many of them decided it was preferable to let people stay and maintain the properties. Often they let delinquent renters stay with the promise of future payment. People who lost their jobs and homes turned first to families and friends for help. If no one could loan or give them money or take them in, they wound up on the road or on the streets. John Steinbeck's *Grapes of Wrath* tells the story of the "Okies" who left the dust bowl in search of work and a better life in California. Unfortunately, few of them found either.

The muddled sun sneaks through the skinny branches of barren trees as rib showing dogs yelp in greeting. A child cries with hunger, continuing the tune he started the night before. Cardboard homes slowly crumble from last night's steady drizzle, while mothers gather the runoff into abandoned bottles to make a weak and tepid pot of coffee. Single men gather around an oil drum fire, swapping stories and curses through rotting teeth. In the distance comes the shrill cackle of someone's well fed rooster . . . Daybreak in Hooverville.[15]

Hoovervilles

Many families lived in cars or thrown together shacks. Whole colonies of shacks and tents grew up on the outskirts of major cities or near city dumps. These shanty towns came to be called "Hoovervilles" in satiric reference to President Hoover, who many blamed for the Depression. Periodically the authorities would tear down the encampments whose abysmal sanitary conditions presented severe health hazards. The residents, mostly single men, would hit the rails or the highways aimlessly searching for a place in the sun.

Crime

There are no reliable figures to accurately tell how much crime increased in the Depression, but many people turned to shoplifting and petty crime out of desperation to feed their families. A Los Angeles study in 1932 observed two distinct classes of criminals: the habitual criminal and the criminal of necessity — the type resulting from the Depression, a particularly unfortunate manifestation of which was the increase in prostitution.[16] Regular prostitutes called these newcomers "Depression Girls," driven into prostitution by economic distress.

The largest increase in crime, however, was in organized crime. Gambling, protection rackets, and bootlegging fueled a tremendous growth in the criminal empires of gangsters like Al Capone. The 18th amendment to the Constitution had outlawed alcohol and provided ample opportunity for organized crime to flourish. Gangsters and speakeasies operated brazenly with the bribed approval of most police forces. The astounding fortunes amassed by leading criminals led to a whole movement that fervently believed that the repeal of Prohibition would single-handedly end the Depression by providing millions of legitimate jobs in a legalized brewing industry. The repeal of Prohibition in 1933 created some jobs, but nowhere near enough to dent the force of the ongoing depression.

Entertainment and recreation

People demoralized by the pressures of a lengthy depression devoured entertainment. Talking movies were a recent development that captivated millions with the antics of the Marx Brothers and Shirley Temple's voyages on the Good Ship Lollipop. Attendance at movies was down overall due to poverty, but nevertheless it was perhaps the most popular form of entertainment throughout the Depression. Radio listening increased tremendously as radio prices declined and families huddled around the receiver for exciting episodes of their favorite serials.

Leisure time increased for people who had lost their jobs or had their hours shortened, but expensive recreation decreased. Participation in sports and athletic programs surged with less expensive public parks, beaches, swimming pools, and tennis courts receiving heavy usage. Public libraries were often jammed as people read the daily newspapers and pored through books to acquire new skills and fill their jobless days with learning and literature.

Various crazes swept the nation; the most popular included miniature golf, handcrafts, recipe collecting, and contract bridge. In 1931, Americans spent $10 million for bridge lessons. Perhaps the oddest craze was the phenomenon of marathon dancing wherein young couples attempted to win prizes by staying awake for days trying to see who could dance the longest. Gambling prospered as people tried to strike it rich without working; games such as keno, bingo, poker, and craps were all popular.

Women

Conditions for working women during the Depression were difficult. Women's wages, which were already 50% lower than men's wages for comparable work, plunged from an average of $45 a week to $10 a week.[17] Many women became their family's major breadwinner, but also continued performing all the household domestic chores. In her popular book published in 1934, *Women Who Work*, Grace Hutchins decried the "double slavery" of both work and housekeeping. She urged women to organize and strike for benefits such as maternity leave and day nurseries.

State legislators across the country enacted laws to curtail the employment of married women, who many felt were taking jobs away from "men who really needed them." In 1932, Section 213 of the Federal Economic Act required that one spouse resign if both worked for the government. Seventy five percent of those resigning were women. Despite these laws, the number of married women in the work force increased by 50% from 1930 to 1940, primarily out of economic necessity.[18]

Although two million working women lost their jobs in the Depression, less women than men were laid off. Only 25% of women were in the work force in 1930, and the occupations they held in the clothing and food industries were much less affected than the male jobs in manufacturing and construction.

Minorities

Minoritites lived in desperate straits throughout the Depression. This country, only sixty years past the abolition of slavery, victimized blacks and other minorities with

Reidsville, Georgia Oct. 19th 1935
. . . They give out the relief supplies here on Wednesday of this week and give us black folks, each one, nothing but a few cans of pickled meat and to white folks they give blankets, bolts of cloth and things like that. . . Yours truly can't sign my name Mr. President, they will beat me up and run me away from here and this is my home.
—Anonymous
(from a letter written to President Roosevelt)[19]

pervasive and systematic racism. Most unions were blatantly racist, and minority workers who held low paying domestic and agricultural jobs were unprotected by New Deal labor reform. Despite their plight, many blacks admired President Roosevelt.

Often the administration and dispersal of relief funds were tainted by racism, making it harder for minorities to obtain the assistance they needed. Indeed, it was only when the worst effects of the Depression began to seep into the white middle class that the government mobilized intensive relief efforts. Perhaps the only advantage many minority groups had during the Depression was a cultural history of helping each other. Working together through minority churches and communities was the only thing that prevented a worst catastrophe among blacks, Native Americans, and Hispanics.

Suicide

The myth of masses of stock brokers committing suicide by jumping out of Wall Street buildings after the crash of 1929 was later disproved. Less than 1% of suicides in New York between October and December of 1929 were directly caused by the stock market crash. In reality the nation's suicide rate grew from a level of 14 per 100,000 people in 1929 to a high of 17.2 per 100,000 in 1932, and then declined to 12 per 100,000 by 1935.[20]

Religion

It is believed that in economic hard times people turn to religion in large numbers. Many religious ministers welcomed the Depression as a sort of spiritual cleansing that would boost church attendance. However, traditional churches saw only small increases in their numbers and large decreases in their contributions.[21] Fundamentalist churches, which were much smaller in the 1930's than they are today, did show steady rises in memberships, beginning in the 1920's and lasting through the Depression. Charismatic figures including Father Coughlin and Amy Semple MacPherson captured a great deal of attention through radio broadcasts and mass meetings. In a time of confusion and despair, they helped fulfill a yearning for simple answers to difficult problems.

Churches experienced financial difficulties that caused them to curtail their social service work. As the Depression wore on and social problems grew to be enormous, church leaders realized they could not begin to address people's needs, and they turned to the government to provide the bulk of relief efforts.

THE RESPONSE OF GOVERNMENT

The Hoover Administration

The initial response to the Depression by the U.S. Government was to use a time honored political technique — namely, pretend it wasn't happening. As late as 1931, President Hoover and his cabinet maintained that the country was just experiencing a temporary economic downturn and that shortly happy days would be here again. Unfortunately, it took ten years and a war for economic happy days to return for millions. At first, Hoover was reluctant to commit any federal government funds to depression relief. He was firmly committed to voluntarism and did not want the federal government to interfere with the responsibility and authority of state and local governments. Eventually it became clear that private charities and state governments had nowhere near the resources needed to alleviate the massive suffering of the jobless, hungry, and homeless. Still, Hoover made only token efforts to help. His lack of action, together with the simplistic but popular notion that the Depression was Hoover's doing, insured Roosevelt's landslide victory in the election of 1932.

Roosevelt and the New Deal

Franklin Delano Roosevelt had been governor of the state of New York. He and the Democrats were swept into office on a tide of popularity stoked by the belief that he would be able to do something to turn the country around. In his inaugural speech on March 4, 1933, Roosevelt promised "action, and action now," in this "dark hour of national life." He added, *"We do not distrust the future of essential democracy. The people of the United States have not failed. In their need they have registered a mandate that they want direct, vigorous action. They have asked me for discipline, and direction under leadership. They have made me the present instrument of their wishes. In the spirit of the gift, I take it."[22]*

Roosevelt immediately went to work turning his words into forceful action. On March 9, 1933 Congress was called, and in the well known Hundred Days (March to July, 1933), 13 vital measures were passed. The Agricultural Adjustment Act was passed in an effort to increase the purchasing power of farmers. The primary result, however, was to decrease crop production, thus increasing prices for farm products. Farmers were paid to keep land out of production, a practice which benefited the large landowners more than small farmers. It benefited tenant farmers and sharecroppers not at all. Provisions that payments were to be passed on to tenants were often circumvented or ignored. The most controversial aspect of the AAA was the plowing under of crops and slaughter of pigs. It was abhorrent to many to destroy food at a time when millions were hungry. The Federal Relief Emergency Act authorized $500 million for unemployment relief. The Federal Emergency Relief Administration (FERA), under the direction of Harry Hopkins, moved quickly to dispense funds to the states for direct relief. Over the next three years the amount spent for relief grew to $1 billion a year, which was approximately 2% of national income, a level not seen before.

The National Industrial Recovery Act (NIRA) provided for massive public works under the Public Works Administration (PWA). Like the Agricultural Adjustment Act, it also gave the federal government unprecedented powers of control over private enterprise. This was fought bitterly by business interests, and eventually (in 1935) the NIRA and AAA were declared unconstitutional by the Supreme Court. This led an angry Roosevelt to initiate an ill-fated attempt to expand the Supreme Court with his own supporters. Here, too, he failed.

The other acts of the Hundred Days included the Securities Exchange Act (to regulate the stock market and protect investors), and the Emergency Banking Act, which allowed the Federal Reserve Bank to issue more money and control credit. Federal Deposit Insurance was created to protect depositors. The Tennessee Valley Authority Act (TVA) undertook the development of flood control, power generation, and reforestation along the Tennessee River. This massive project protected the land from private business exploitation and was so successful it led to a demand for more construction of power sites around the country.

The major effect of Roosevelt's strong action was to restore people's confidence and discourage defeatism. Statements such as, "We have nothing to fear but fear itself" were taken to heart by millions of Americans, and hope was kindled. Roosevelt communicated that he cared for the plight of the common people. The fact that many of the hopes he raised were not fulfilled was secondary to a nation that needed a spark of enthusiasm and positivity.

Some of Roosevelt's most ambitious projects were thwarted by businessmen who particularly opposed public works employment projects which they feared would make it difficult for them to hire labor at low wages. Because of the problems of the NIRA, Harry Hopkins and the public works programs were shifted to the newly created Civil Works Administration (CWA) in the winter of 1933-34. In a short time the CWA initiated 400,000 projects and employed four million people. Under political pressure from business interests, the program was shelved in the spring of 1934.

Public works programs came back in 1935, again under the direction of Hopkins, in the form of the Works Progress Administration. It was funded by an Emergency Relief Appropriation of $4.8 billion, a huge sum that represented 10% of the previous year's entire federal income. At its height, it gave jobs to only 25% of the unemployed. Nevertheless, its accomplishments were impressive, including constructing or rebuilding more than 200,000 buildings and bridges and 600,000 miles of roads.[23] Not only did it fund laborers, but it also provided jobs for professionals, including lawyers, architects, artists, actors, and writers.

Despite the economic stimulus provided by the WPA, the scope of the program was drastically curtailed after the election of 1936, leading many to feel that its primary purpose had been to defuse political discontent rather than to alleviate suffering. Due to his skill at defusing dissent many credit Roosevelt and the New Deal with saving the existing capitalist system by preventing extremism of the right (fascism) and of the left (communism) from taking hold in the United States.

Other important measures enacted during Roosevelt's tenure as president included the Wagner Act of 1935, which established fair labor and collective bargaining practices, and the establishment of a minimum wage, which for the first time protected the rights of working people. The Social Security Act of 1935 instituted unemployment insurance as well as provided aid to senior citizens and dependent children. These measures had been proposed for many years but had always met stiff opposition from business interests. The destitution of the unemployed and the elderly during the Depression eventually overcame objections that it was socialistic. Initial benefits were low, but over time Social Security expanded into the huge program it is today. Never before in United States history had any government, state or federal, acted so directly to relieve economic distress. The philosophy of letting the market seek its own level had prevailed, and previous presidents like Hoover had eschewed responsibility for making wholesale changes in order to relieve suffering and stimulate the economy. Roosevelt was willing to take the risk and tackle issues that had never been addressed. After an initial aversion to budget deficits, he was forced to finance New Deal projects with deficit spending. This step proved necessary to decrease the unprecedented unemployment and suffering of American citizens.

Every depression has as many stories as there are people who lived through it. What some experienced as a minor inconvenience was for others a life threatening nightmare. No one who lived through a depression was totally untouched, but the degree of hardship varied dramatically. A depression brings out the best in those who sacrifice to help the needy and the worst in others who retreat into fear and selfishness. Seek out anyone you know that has memories of their life in the last depression. Let them tell you in their own words what it was like: for themselves, their family, and the world. Ask them questions about areas of particular concern to you and get their recommendations on what you and your family can do to get ready for coping with a depression.

Endnotes

1. Jeane Westin, *Making Do* (Chicago: Follett, 1976), p. 320.
2. Quoted in D.R. McCoy, *Calvin Coolidge: The Quiet President* (New York, 1967), p. 392.
3. U.S. Department of Commerce, *U.S. Income and Output* (1959), p. 130.
4. Cabell Phillips, *From the Crash to the Blitz, 1929—1939; the New York Times Chronicle of American Life* (New York: Macmillan, 1969), p. xii.
5. Robert S. McElvaine, *Down and Out in the Great Depression* (Chapel Hill, North Carolina: University of North Carolina Press, 1983), p. 18.
6. Walter de la Mare, *The Slum Child*, 1933.
7. John A. Garraty, *The Great Depression* (San Diego: Harcourt, Brace, Jovanovich, 1986), p. 110.
8. Paul Lazarfield, *Marienthal: The Sociography of an Unemployed Community* (Chicago: University of Chicago Press, 1971), pp. 52-54.
9. Walter Greenwood, *Love on the Dole*, (London, 1969), p. 169.
10. Arthur Schlesinger, *Age of Roosevelt*, (Boston: Houghton Mifflin, 1957), vol. 1, p. 241.
11. Lester V. Chandler, *America's Greatest Depression 1929-1941*, (New York: Harper and Row, 1970), p. 55.
12. Chandler, p. 59.
13. Chandler, p. 62.
14. Will Carlton, *Alliance Herald*, (Stafford, Kansas, May 29, 1980).
15. Mark Friedman, 1988.
16. Throsten Sellin, *Research Memorandum on Crime in the Depression*, (New York: Arno Press, 1972), p. 45.
17. Westin, p. 164
18. Judith Selander, *As Minority Becomes Majority*, (Westport: Greenwood Press, 1983), p. 61.
19. McElvaine, p. 83
20. *American Demographics*, October, 1987, p. 14.
21. Samuel C. Kincheloe, *Research Memorandum on Religion in the Depression* (New York: Arno Press, 1972), p. 35.
22. Marion Yass, *The Great Depression* (London: Wayland Publishers, 1970), p. 93.
23. McElvaine, p. 25.

Chapter

4

The Shape of Things to Come

SIGNS OF CHANGE

The coming depression will dramatically affect all facets of life. The baby boom generation has grown up in a time of relative prosperity. To most of us, the last depression is just a story told by grandpa or a scary time we read about. When the rug gets pulled out from under the secure world of material wealth and values, we will make a traumatic adjustment. Let's look at some of the changes that will take place.

Another crash?

The wheels that are bringing the depression are already in motion. A gradually growing percentage of the population is experiencing depression-like conditions on a daily basis; the U.S. has a poverty rate of 20% and two million homeless people. A significant event paralleling the stock market crash of October 29, 1929 may be identified as the start of the next depression, but in all likelihood the decline will be well under way before then. The most probable source for a focal event is in Japan, where stocks, even after the crash of October 1987, are highly overvalued. Another huge crash in the Japanese Nikei Stock Exchange could trigger an immediate domino effect on stock markets around the world, as Japanese investors liquidate holdings in the U.S. and Europe in order to cover their losses.

Consumer spending down, defaults up

Look for declining consumer spending to herald a U.S. depression. Individual consumers fuel two-thirds of the GNP, and a significant decrease in consumption will lead to increasing layoffs as factories see a decreasing demand for their products. Other danger signals to watch for include defaults by major debtor nations. The international banking system is extremely tenuous, and a wave of developing world debt repudiation could knock Humpty Dumpty right off the wall, where he is precariously balanced.

Don't worry, be happy

At the beginning of the depression, expect political and business leaders to caution the public not to worry. Predictions of a temporary recession will abound, and conventional wisdom will state that it is part of the natural business cycle. You will hear, "Don't worry, our built-in safeguards prevent the recurrence of 1930's style depression." Don't believe these predictions. President Herbert Hoover, his Secretary of the Treasury, Andrew Mellon, and business leaders said all of the same reassuring things in 1930. No president wants to be known as the new Hoover. Whoever is in office when the depression comes will go to great lengths to ignore the deafening sounds of economic collapse.

Business as usual

Businesses will try to hang on as long as possible, in the belief that a turnaround is just ahead. Large corporations, in particular, will wait as long as they can before undertaking massive layoffs. Smaller corporations, whose pockets are not as deep and are more market sensitive, will cutback drastically as soon as their business declines for two quarters in a row. Unionized corporations and industries will keep their employees longer and use the evidence of severe losses as leverage to force unions to renegotiate existing contracts. This will give management the leeway to layoff many and slash the wages of those who remain. Chapter Seven will detail those industries and fields that will suffer the most and those that will be hit less hard. In general, as we saw in the preceding chapter, the non-durable goods industries including food, clothes, and energy will decline much less than the durable goods industries including mining, manufacturing, and construction.

Unemployment, discontent

Social discontent and the call for massive government spending to meet the needs of the jobless, homeless, and hungry will grow with unemployment. Unemployment benefits, currently running for a maximum of 26 weeks, will be extended, like they were in the recession of 1978. Public employment will be urged and eventually enacted to provide jobs for some of the millions of unemployed. Hopefully, the program will be better planned and administrated than the ill fated CETA (Comprehensive Employment and Training Act) jobs program of the late 70's and early 80's. This program was marred by poor administration, make-work jobs, and political patronage.

In the Depression of the 1930's, the unemployed blamed themselves for being out of work. In the coming depression, the unemployed will blame anyone else, with the government and big business bearing the brunt of dissatisfaction. Look for the unemployed to be extremely vocal in their demands for relief. The jobless will not worry about where the money is going to come to fund their demands, but politicians will. They are likely to resist the obvious solution of taxing the wealthy, in the belief that this will hamper investment and economic recovery. Also, elected officials more often project and protect the interests of those who finance their campaigns. Politicians who fail to respond to the growing demands of the needy will likely find *themselves* out of jobs come the next election. They need only look at Roosevelt's landslide defeat of Hoover in the election of 1932 to see their eventual fate.

Farmers — more of the same

Farmers and farm communities will see abject conditions. The current hard times in the heartland will get even worse as crop prices fall even further. Farm loans will be seriously delinquent, and even more farm banks will teeter and fall. Again, look for a demand for government assistance. The FDIC (Federal Deposit Insurance Corporation) will be implored to bail out these and the other failing banks. However, without the infusion of billions of dollars, the FDIC will be able to help only a small percentage of the banks that need it.

Helping farmers directly through price supports will be urged. The most humane solution will be for the government to purchase extensive food crops for distribution to the hungry, much as is done now through the food commodities program that distributes milk, butter, cheese, flour, rice, and other staples. Continued subsidies of cash crops such as tobacco will make little sense in a time when people are starving. A key question is how much of government aid to agriculture will go to large corporate farms as happened in the 1930's, and how much will go to smaller family farms?

Our daily bread

Don't expect to see massive food shortages, at least in the first few years of the depression. There will be plenty of food available, just little money to purchase it with. Thus stockpiling of food in preparation for the depression may not be necessary. Rather it is recommended to save money, so you will be able to purchase the food you need at lower prices. The food stamp program, which currently serves 20 million people, will have to expand exponentially to meet the needs of what could be 40 to 60 million people. Community food banks will be stretched to the limit in trying to meet these needs. Expect to see the return of bread lines to serve those unable to receive other assistance. The soup kitchens of today will have to become the mass feeding stations of tomorrow.

Home sweet . . .

The lack of affordable housing has led increasing numbers of the jobless and working poor to the streets in search of shelter. Massive layoffs during the depression will exacerbate this problem beyond belief. A recent study from the Massachussets Institute of Technology projects that nearly 19 million people will be homeless by the end of the century. That projection is not based upon a full scale depression like we will experience. Through evictions, foreclosures, and lack of adequate government subsidized housing 30 million people may be homeless during the depression. Again the problem will be one of purchasing power, not lack of dwelling space. Those who can will turn to friends and relatives, and the practice of doubling and tripling up will increase tremendously. Where zoning laws prohibit this practice, the laws will have to be changed or ignored.

Industries

Areas of the country particularly hard hit will be those that are dependent on one or two primary industries. Single industry or company cities like Detroit, Michigan and Gary, Indiana will be like ghost towns compared to the present. Towns and cities dependent on mining and heavy industry will suffer severe slumps that will permeate all facets of life. Those who can will leave in droves seeking a better life in better climates and job markets. Just as a better life in California eluded the "Okies" in the 30's, newcomers to the depression era sun belt will find the promised land fulfills few of its promises. Those who stay will be dependent on private and public assistance to survive.

Health

The quality of medical care available will decline sharply. Millions of workers will lose their health insurance when they lose their jobs. Medicaid and state and municipal medical programs for the indigent will not be able to serve all of those in need. Look for a steady deterioration in children's nutrition and an increase in low birth weight babies as the economy crashes. Studies from around the world show that in times of economic decline children suffer.

Entertainment

Look for a boom in a wide variety of low cost entertainment as the nation attempts to dull the pain of economic distress. The current celebrity mania will increase. The media and public will create larger than life television, movie, music, and sports stars. Their glamorous lives will thrill and delight millions, many of whom are mired in hardship and misery. New entertainment crazes will sweep the country, capturing the fancy of many.

Nostalgia will become even more popular than it is now, as hard times reinforce an aching desire for a return to "the good old days." Previous depressions have brought a greater conservatism in fashion, music, and sexual mores. Hem lines traditionally come down along with the Gross National Product. The coming depression will bring a highly contrasting mixture of conservative and avant garde expression. Many will be looking for the tried and true, but others will seek the most outlandish and potentially degrading forms of expression. The emergence of skin-heads and punks in contemporary depressed Great Britain is an example of this.

Culturally, it will lead to an increase in pseudo-culture — mass produced entertainment of the lowest common denominator that is geared only towards commercial success. A disregard for true artistic and expansive expression will be epitomized by network television and mindless movies. Look for exploitative entertainment with sexual and violent themes to flourish during the depression, as long as its purveyors can make a buck.

Good things to look for

A positive result of the depression will be a tremendous growth in self-help projects. Food cooperatives, community gardens, labor exchanges, and collective endeavors of all kinds will find willing participants among both low-income and middle class people. The "every man and woman for him or herself" philosophy of our current society will be impractical for many. By pooling human energy and resources, many will be better able to meet their needs. The government will be wise to support these efforts. In the long run, many more people will be able to survive through working together and less will need welfare.

Another inspiring aspect of our new depressionary world will be a tremendous outpouring of compassion and assistance for those in need. Many will feel compelled to relieve the suffering they see every day, both around them and on television. The true heroes of the depression will give tirelessly of themselves to feed, clothe, and shelter those in need. There will be a tremendous shortage of jobs, but no lack of work. Anyone who is healthy and has their own basic needs met will have the ability and the responsibility to help others in their community. The real spirit of the American people will shine brightly through those who use their time to act strongly to improve the lot of those less fortunate.

It's worldwide

Our present economy is a global one. Foreigners own large blocks of real estate, stock, and industry in America, and Americans own large parts of the developed and developing world. The depression will be global and all will suffer. Internationally, through multiplier effects, a 1% drop in the United States GNP leads to a 10% drop in a developing country. Countries dependent on exports to the West will suffer greatly.

The oil-exporting countries of the Middle East will be among the hardest hit, due to lack of economic diversity. Economic decline will increase global political tensions between the developed and the developing world. Calls for economic protectionism will mount as more American workers lose their jobs, despite the fact that the protectionist Smoot-Hawley Act of 1930 is generally blamed for making the depression of the 30's deeper and longer.

Superpowers will be forced to curtail defense spending in the face of mounting expenditures for human needs. The cold war between the Soviet Union and the United States will be temporarily defused, but the underlying tension will not dissipate in the face of economic adversity. The looming menace of World War III is not pleasant to contemplate, but keep in mind that previous depressions have ended with wars.

The mythical safety net

Popular mythology holds that since Roosevelt's New Deal we are protected with a government safety net. To prevent economic collapse, we have the power of the Federal Reserve to manipulate the money supply and interest rates. To prevent stock market collapse, we have stringent margin requirements and the Securities Exchange Commission (SEC). To prevent the wholesale collapse of banks, we have federal deposit insurance and a willingness of the government to prop up ailing, overextended, and mismanaged institutions. To prevent widespread social misery, we have unemployment insurance, social security, food stamps, and Medicare.

All of those safeguards will prove inadequate. The Federal Reserve existed before the 1930's, but did little to prevent or ameliorate the effects of the depression. The SEC started in 1933, but could not prevent or lessen the market meltdown of October 1987. The Federal Deposit Insurance Corporation (FDIC) reserves cover only 1.1% of all deposits, leaving it unable to withstand the flood of bank failures the depression will bring.

In the beginning of the depression unemployment insurance, social security, food stamps, and Medicare/Medicaid will blunt the worst effects of joblessness, but will be rapidly overwhelmed after the economic collapse. Many people are unable to utilize these programs. Many of the current two million homeless fall through the cracks of traditional government assistance due to the lack of a permanent address and shortages of low income housing. During the depression, millions more will be left out of the relief programs that government and private agencies will have to offer. The ropes of the safety net will be just too wide to catch all those who are falling.

A crisis of leadership

As more people become destitute, the pressure for social change will escalate to a level not seen since the Revolutionary War. The desperate armies of the jobless, hungry, and homeless will make the Civil Rights and Vietnam War protests seem puny. Their demands for assistance will join the pleas of banks, farmers, industry, and the military for a monetary balm to their feverish state. How will a government already on the verge of bankruptcy be able to respond to these pleas? It cannot. Those that apply the most pressure will get the most relief.

A major determinant of how effectively that pressure is applied will be leadership. In depressions charismatic leaders rise to harness the undirected energy of the suffering masses. In Germany that leader was Hitler; in Italy it was Mussolini. Fortunately, in the United States, Franklin Delano Roosevelt (FDR) was able to capture the imagination and kindle the hopes of the American people. Thus we avoided the despotism and tyranny of the right or the left that shackled many other countries. However, as Roosevelt was unable to turn the country around, the popularity of Senator Huey P. Long of Louisiana soared. The "Kingfish" proposed sweeping changes in taxation and distribution of wealth that brought him an extremely wide following. Had he not been assassinated, he may have defeated Roosevelt in 1936 or 1940.

Who will be the next FDR, "Kingfish," or der Fuhrer? No one can say now, but strong men and women will emerge to galvanize both public discontent and a yearning for solutions to the complex problems of the depression. These leaders may be politicians, but more likely they will be religious leaders who are able to couch their solutions in spiritual terminology that speaks to people's deepest fears and aspirations. The future of our country and the world will depend on how much love, compassion, and humility the emerging leaders truly feel. If they are demagogic, self-serving, and narrow minded, we are in for a world of hurt with no end — or the ultimate end — in sight. The well wishers of humanity will have to mobilize to prevent tyrannical despots from stepping into the leadership vacuum.

INDIVIDUALS AND FAMILIES — SOME SCENARIOS

What will the depression be like for you and your family? No one can say for sure, but if you do nothing to prepare you are likely to suffer more. Realistically, most people, with the exception of those reading this book and acting on its recommendations, will do little to get ready. Those who are not prepared will have to scramble to adapt to a drastically changed world. Some sample fictional scenarios of how some may adapt follow:

Sam
Sam followed his father into the steel mills of Riverton. Right out of high school, he got his first job and during his ten years with the company he rose to the position of supervisor. Life in the mill was hard.

The heat and smoke seared his lungs, and every day his backache flared up. But he felt he was well rewarded. He and his wife Pat saved and bought a three bedroom brick bungalow after his first five years on the job.

When the depression came, their two daughters, Judy and Susan, were seven and nine. Their youngest, Bobby, had recently turned three. Four hundred lost their jobs in the first wave of layoffs, but Sam, with his ten years of seniority, stayed on. After three months, the expected turn around in the steel industry didn't materialize. Five hundred more were laid off, including Sam.

He was worried, but in his ten years he had seen two recessions and the laid off workers were always called back when things picked up. For the first few months, he and Pat cut down on buying new clothes for the kids. They got hand me downs from friends and her sister Sarah. After six months Sam's unemployment benefits ran out. Sarah earned a little money with a part time job as a cashier at the local supermarket, but it wasn't enough to make the mortgage payment. They gradually spent their savings over the next six months waiting for the turn around at the mill that never came.

They ended up moving in with his folks, who had a small frame house in town. Sam and Sarah and the three kids shared one room in the basement and the living room couch. Between Sarah's part time work, his parents' social security, and Sam's occasional odd job they survived. The kids learned to live without new clothes and toys.

After three years the plant had four employees, all security guards protecting it from vandalism. One day Sam and his kids went out to look at the plant. Weeds had reclaimed most of the massive parking lot, jagged fragments of broken windows caught the glint of the sun, a guard dog behind a ten foot barbed wire fence snarled at them, and they quietly walked home.

Judy

Judy lived in the lower middle class town of Edgedale, California with her two children, 5 year old Peter and 3 year old Valerie. Since her divorce, she supported her family through a job as a receptionist at a small insurance company paying $5 an hour and sporadic child support from her ex-husband Carl. Her take home pay of $688 a month almost paid for her one bedroom apartment, food for the family, and Valerie's daycare. The $150 Carl sent every other month helped make up the shortfall on the rent, paid for clothes and shoes for the children, visits to the doctor, and an occasional family outing to see a kid's movie at the local mall.

When the depression came, the insurance company lost a lot of business, laid off half their agents, and asked Valerie to cut back her hours to half time. She looked for another full time job, but nobody was hiring. She reluctantly agreed to go half time, with a take home pay of $375.

Judy took Valerie out of day care, and put her in the care of the 15 year old who lived down the hall. She applied for food stamps and was told there was at least a three month wait and that those with no income at all had priority. The checks from Carl stopped coming.

Judy's father had died when she was 19 and her mother died six months after Peter was born. Her only sibling, Frank, hadn't spoken with her in 13 years. Carl's parents wanted nothing to do with Peter and Valerie. When Valerie got whooping cough, the last of Judy's money went to the doctor and the pharmacy. She got enough food from the local food bank to last till the end of the month, but they told her she could only use their services one time. At the end of the month, she barely had enough to pay the rent. The next two months she didn't. Eviction proceedings were initiated, and after another two months she and the children found their meager belongings in the street. A neighbor had storage space to keep a few boxes of their stuff, but no one had room for them.

Judy used her next paycheck to buy an old beat-up car for $150. They moved into the car and bought just enough gas to move it from place to place when someone told them to go. Judy slept in the front seat; Valerie and Peter shared the back. On Sundays the car sputtered to reach the beach. Valerie and Peter built a house out of sand every week and every Sunday night, the tide rolled in and washed it away.

Todd

Todd worked as a stock broker at an up and coming brokerage in the Denver Tech Center. Every day he moved thousands of shares of stock for his clients, many of whom he met at the trendy health club he belonged to in Cherry Creek. Every weekend in the winter he drove his leased Saab to Vail or Copper Mountain to ski and party. When Wall Street crashed all his clients wanted Todd to cash them out and fast. He did, and many took huge losses, Todd included. After collecting his sales commissions, he was left with $15,000 in cash.

"Hey, no problem," he thought. " The market will come back." After a month, Todd and his fellow brokers thought they smelled the bottom — a great time to buy. Todd took $10,000 of the $12,000 he had left and invested it in blue chips — the safest way to go. The bottom proved to be a false one and his $12,000 dwindled to $5,000 and falling after two months. Two months behind on rent, he cashed out. Three months later the health club membership was voided for non-payment and one sad day in August the leasing company came for the Saab.

Todd grew increasingly more depressed as the market traded at a snail's pace and mostly downhill. He lost the apartment and moved in with one of his buddies. They sat around a lot, drinking beer, watching the Denver Broncos on TV, and scheming about where they could scrape up the cash to take a flyer on gold futures. They never did come up with the money and it's just as well — it turned out to be a losing trade. After six months, he and his buddy lost the apartment and Todd moved to Iowa to help out on his aunt and uncle's farm. He didn't have any money, but he always had enough to eat. Hard as he tried, though, he never could get the tractor to accelerate like his old Saab.

Dorothy

Dorothy grew up on the south side of Chicago, the third of four children. Her dad directed an "El" train on the Howard Street line and her mom took the Chicago and Northwestern up to the North Shore three days a week to work as a maid. Dorothy worked her way through the University of Illinois-Chicago Circle by waiting tables at a popular pizza place. With her degree in social work, she got a job as a caseworker at the Cook County Department of Social Services.

Five years of bureaucracy, red tape, paperwork, and budget cuts left her frustrated and burnt out. Then the depression came and things got worse. The sordid living conditions of her clients shocked and appalled her. When she saw how little the county was able to do for them, she quit. She had saved enough money to live on for a few years, especially at depression prices.

She called a meeting with some of her friends and former clients who lived in the neighborhood. Together they decided to pool some of their money and skills and see what could be done to improve the situation. They researched a number of options and decided to start a housing cooperative. They visited the Bethel Housing Coop on the west side, and were offered all the technical assistance and guidance they needed. After six months and struggles with landlords, bankers, and the city, their housing cooperative was born. Fifteen families moved in and in time renovated the old brownstone building into a place they could be proud of.

As they learned to work together, they found new strength in sharing and combining their individual talents and resources. They used that strength to expand into a small food cooperative and an appliance repair cooperative. As they struggled and achieved some success, they were able to set up a neighborhood food bank to feed many families and help them set up their own small cooperatives.

Dorothy spent the rest of the depression working with others to help them find their own strength in working cooperatively. She was never financially well off, but she felt her life to be as rich as it could possibly be.

Chapter

5

Your Financial Future

KING CASH

You support your lifestyle with money from four basic sources: work, assets and savings, credit, and the government. In this chapter you will discover why, during the coming depression, your savings may well be your only source of money.

In the coming depression, many financial empires built on paper foundations will crumble. As faith in the financial system dwindles, fortunes backed by highly leveraged transactions in real estate, stocks, commodities futures, and options will become worthless. In the coming depression, as in almost every previous depression, CASH will be KING.

A deflationary depression will mean that money disappears from circulation and prices shrink with industrial output and jobs. Between late 1929 and 1932 all commodities prices shrank by 45%; 57% of U.S. farm harvests vanished; and the average of reported economic indicators showed a remarkable 30% shrinkage.[1,2]

You can expect to see similar conditions, or worse, during the depression of the 1990's. Prices on homes and cars will tumble, along with those of microwaves and VCRs. Saving wisely between now and the start of this depression will put you in a better position to support your family, to have cash available when prices drop and money is scarce, and to be able to help others who are less prepared for the cash squeeze.

Sidney Weinberg, a former senior partner with the Goldman-Sachs investment firm, commenting on the Depression of the 1930's said, "Most of the net worth of people today is in values. They haven't got it in cash. In a panic, values go down regardless of worth." Further, referring to people's opinion that their net worth is based on the equity in their homes and other monetary values, he added, "But it's all on paper."[3] The cash squeeze will manifest in three ways. First, credit will disappear. Jobs will rapidly follow and, for those still working, wages will shrink. Then the shaky banking and financial system will deteriorate.

NO CREDIT AVAILABLE

The 1980's has seen an unprecedented rise in credit and overall indebtedness. The total national indebtedness leaped from $4.7 trillion to $8.2 trillion between the end of 1980 and the end of 1985.[4] Not only are we a debtor nation and a nation of debtors, but corporations, the federal government and most of the countries in the world share this growing addiction to credit. In the crash that precedes the depression, this seemingly endless pool of credit will disappear like the mirage it actually is.

Credit is a vote of confidence. When great depressions appear, confidence in the debtor's implicit promise to repay later vanishes — along with the nation's money supply. In the first three months after the crash of 19, one half of the banks' and two thirds of the United States' money supply disappeared.[5]

When banks have no money, businesses and farmers do not get loans; workers take pay cuts or receive notice; credit disappears; confidence in the system diminishes. As the house of cards that is our financial system begins to tumble, you will no longer be able to get loans from the bank or finance company. All those hard to resist offers of the latest pre-approved credit cards will stop filling your mailbox. When you have no money coming in where can you turn to finance your lifestyle?

YOUR JOB: HERE TODAY . . . GONE TOMORROW?

The logical and most secure source of cash for most of us is a job. Most Americans count on having a relatively steady income. This is the security we use to pay for the necessities and luxuries of life. We use the future earnings from this job as collateral to run up large credit card, installment, and automobile loan debts.

As the next depression deepens, steady employment will disappear for many Americans. It is true, as described in Chapter Seven, that some fields and careers will be more secure than others, but on the whole few people will be guaranteed to hold their current jobs for the duration of the depression. Peak unemployment during the Thirties passed one-third of the nation's work force. Auto workers, attorneys, nurses, teachers, coal miners, waitresses, actors, stockbrokers and bank executives may have to face getting up in the morning without a paying job waiting for them.

For those still working, salary cuts may make it harder, or impossible, to meet their current obligations. Today millions of workers earning the minimum wage live in poverty. During the 1990's, these workers will have lots of company.

YOUR RICH UNCLE SAM?

All indications are that the coming depression will see more people thrown out of work than the last depression, with slim prospects of getting another job soon. It took a change of administrations and four years for the federal government to take decisive tangible action in the last depression. Presumably the government and Federal Reserve Board have much tighter controls over the economy and would not allow as deep a crash as the 1929 to 1932 disaster. But there are forces at work that inspire little confidence in this economic safety net. For example, the government has shown itself willing to run up huge deficits in order to meet increased demands for national defense, human services, and entitlement programs.

This generosity has its price. Some four hundred federal entitlement programs ranging from veteran's benefits and Social Security to medical research, Food Stamps and home loan guarantees require subsidies in our current economy. By 1983, the commitments from these entitlement programs and others reached the point where, in the event of economic crisis, the federal government would be obligated to provide over ten trillion dollars in payments.[6] This does not include depression relief payments. When you need the federal government most, it may be paralyzed for months or years before it can provide relief.

IT'S MONEY IN THE BANK ... or is it?

Even if you have enough saved up to ride out the worst of the storm, there is also unpleasant news. Your certificate of deposit, money market fund, bank or stock market-based I.R.A., and passbook savings account may be less secure than you think. Severe depressions leave financial institutions in such bad shape that there is literally no bank or savings and loan that is secure enough for the typical saver to safely store funds and expect subsequent access to them.

Every severe depression comes as a shock to the leadership of the country when it occurs. In February of 1932, during the original hearings to gain federal backing for bank accounts, members of the Banking Committee shocked other House members by revealing that the nation's banking system was in such bad shape that details could not be given to the full house — or the public.[7] By December of that year, barely two years after the start of the Great Depression, over 4,000 banks had failed.[8] In the early 1930's, the savings of millions of people were wiped out completely.

We now have the Federal Deposit Insurance Corporation (FDIC) and the Federal Savings and Loan Corporation (FSLIC) to insure our savings and checking deposits up to $100,000. Bank deposits totalled $2 trillion in 1985. The FDIC backs a mere 1.19 percent of this money with $18 billion.[9] Twenty-four percent of the nation's bank deposits are not covered by any federal insurance. The trillion dollars on deposit at Savings and Loans are backed by the FSLIC. During the next depression, your line of credit, your earning power, and your bank account may quickly become history. The next chapter will cover the most secure places for your money.

SAVING — THE SOLUTION TO THE COMING CASH SQUEEZE

The solution to the lack of cash in the depression is to save every possible cent you can between now and the crash. Developing the savings habit may take a drastic reordering of your priorities and require a great deal of sacrifice. In the United States we save only 3% of our income. This pales in comparison to the savings rate of 20% in Japan and 15% in Europe.[10,11] In order to save enough money to ensure your family's survival through the depression, you will have to budget to save at a higher rate. Later in this chapter detailed budgets will be presented to help you figure out how to do this.

Our tax system discourages saving and encourages us to borrow. The Tax Reform Act of 1986, by removing installment credit deductions and leaving mortgage loans deductible, has actually decreased U.S. savings by allowing tax credit for the use of home equity loans to buy consumer goods.

More significant than tax laws has been the general mood of materialism and the desire for instant gratification. Post World War II baby boomers, raised in a time of relative prosperity, have enthusiastically bought more and more consumer goods. We have been quick to pull out our credit cards and pay 18% to 21% interest on our purchases, rather than waiting until we have enough money saved to pay cash. Instant gratification is a mania that television and advertising reinforce.

When the depression hits, the shaky foundation of our mass consumption economy will be exposed. The desire to consume for its own sake and to seek happiness through material things can be reversed through a program of saving that deemphasizes credit and reorders our priorities. The following section will help you examine your priorities and measure what it takes to guarantee that you have the financial resources to provide for them.

CASH AND SURVIVAL

In a time of scarce jobs, cash, and credit, survival will be the number one priority. In developing a savings plan, keep in mind how much you will need to meet the basic human survival needs of food, shelter, clothing, medical care, and energy. In our culture, transportation is also a

1. DEPRESSION SURVIVAL BUDGET

Survival Expense	Monthly Cost	(x12) Annual Cost
Food	$_____	$_____
Shelter Includes rent or mortgage + insurance + taxes	_____	_____
Clothing Think of survival needs, not fashion needs	_____	_____
Medical Care Includes insurance premium, deductible, prescription drugs, equipment, etc.	_____	_____
Energy Household utilities including gas, electric, oil, water	_____	_____
Transportation	_____	_____
Total (Survival Figure)	$_____	$_____

factor in basic survival.

Fill in your current costs for the expenses listed in the chart above. These necessities represent the basic survival needs for your family during the coming depression. Use current prices, realizing that some prices will likely decline.

ASSETS

Your *total available assets* will have a direct bearing on the total amount you must save. Available assets include liquid assets, immediately marketable assets, life insurance cash values, certificate of deposits, savings bonds, mutual funds, bonds, personal assets, collectibles and automobiles. Home equities and other values are not shown below because in a depression they rapidly vanish. On Chart 2 write down the

```
┌─────────────────────────────────────────────────────────────┐
│                    2.  AVAILABLE ASSETS                       │
│                                                               │
│   1.  Liquid Assets                                           │
│         a.  Savings/Checking              $_____         │
│                                                               │
│         b.  48 hr. (or less) money accounts  _____       │
│                                                               │
│         c.  Other                           _____        │
│                                                               │
│   2.  Marketable Assets                                       │
│         a.  Stocks                          _____         │
│                                                               │
│         b.  Bonds                           _____         │
│                                                               │
│         c.  Mutual Funds                    _____         │
│                                                               │
│         d.  Commodities                     _____         │
│                                                               │
│         e.  Other                           _____         │
│                                                               │
│   3.  Life Insurance                        _____         │
│                                                               │
│   4.  Certificates of deposit               _____         │
│                                                               │
│   5.  U.S. Savings Bonds                    _____         │
│                                                               │
│   6.  Collectibles                          _____         │
│                                                               │
│   7.  Automobile Equity                     _____         │
│                                                               │
│   8.  Any other personal asset you will be                    │
│       able to instantly liquidate for cash  _____         │
│                                                               │
│            Total Liquid Assets            $_____          │
└─────────────────────────────────────────────────────────────┘
```

amount these items are worth.

Take your yearly Survival Figure (from Chart 1), and subtract the amount of total available Liquid Assets (see Liquid Assets above). The difference between these two numbers is the amount of money you must save, in order to have sufficient funds to survive four years of a depression without assistance from the government, family, friends, or private charitable organizations.

Survival Figure minus Liquid Assets = Savings Needed

HOW TO SAVE

The figure you came up with by subtracting your Liquid Assets from your Survival Figure is, for most people, a significant amount of money. You may well be asking yourself, "How am I supposed to come up with that kind of money on my salary?" For many of us, it will be difficult to save enough in the time remaining before the depression begins. However, you may be surprised at just how much you can save, if you implement some of the suggestions that follow. Chapters Six and Seven will present ways to earn additional income, to augment these savings.

You may not be content to live at this minimal subsistence level. If you expect to live at a higher level, add expenses for telephone, entertainment, restaurant meals, non-survival transportation, a higher clothing allowance, travel, recreation, and any other expenses you consider important to your lifestyle.

In making your plans remember that many of the people you know will not be in a position to support themselves or their families. You may want to include as a budgeted expense, money to help others — including relatives, friends, and the homeless and hungry. Helping others in need is our common responsibility and should not be left to the government — which may not be in the position to do so. The coming depression will give ample opportunity for us to demonstrate our true level of caring.

BUDGETING

Having a budget is the single best way to save money. Surprisingly, only 15% of American families have a written monthly budget that they follow. Developing and following a tight budget that allocates specific amounts for saving will ensure that money will be available when the depression comes.

A detailed income and expense budget form follows. Note that there are three columns to the right of each expense item. Use a five step process to plan for maximum saving:

Step 1. Fill out your current actual monthly expenses in Column 1.
Step 2. Read through the saving suggestions on pages 55 and 56 and write out your own.
Step 3. Then fill out a projected budget in Column 2 that reflects a lower amount in every possible area, except in savings. (Note that the starred expense categories represent non-essential items that will be more easily reducible).
Step 4. Subtract Column 2 from Column 1 and enter these results in Column 3. These are your additional monthly savings. Total them.
Step 5. Add the additional monthly savings plus the line item on savings

plus the amount of difference between income and expenses to get your total amount of monthly savings. It should be a significant amount. This will require some austerity now, but the money you save will make your life much easier during the depression, when money is very hard to find.

Chart 3. Family Budget for Maximum Savings

Monthly Income

Salary(ies)—including bonuses

    You   _____

    Your Spouse   _____

    Other   _____

    Total Salaries $_____

Investment Income

    Interest   _____

    Dividends   _____

    Real estate   _____

    Realized capital gains   _____

    Other investment income _____

    Total Investment Income $_____

Other Income $_____

A. Total Monthly Income $_____

Living, Household, And Personal Expenses

Routine Monthly Living Expenses	**Present**	minus	**New Budget**	=	**Savings**
Food					
Groceries	_____		_____		_____

	Present minus	New Budget =	Savings
*Restaurants & fast food	_____	_____	_____
Total Food Costs	$_____	_____	_____

Home

Rent/Mortgage	_____	_____	_____
Homeowners/renters insurance	_____	_____	_____
*Home improvements	_____	_____	_____
Condo or homeowner's fees	_____	_____	_____
Other housing costs	_____	_____	_____
Total Housing Costs	$_____	_____	_____

Utilities

Gas	_____	_____	_____
Electricity	_____	_____	_____
Telephone (- *long distance)	_____	_____	_____
Water/sewage	_____	_____	_____
Garbage Removal	_____	_____	_____
Total Utilities	$_____	_____	_____

Clothing

Purchase	_____	_____	_____
Laundry/cleaning	_____	_____	_____
Total Clothing	$_____	_____	_____

Transportation

Car loan payment	_____	_____	_____
Automobile insurance	_____	_____	_____
Gas and oil	_____	_____	_____

	Present minus	New Budget =	Savings
Repair/maintenance	_____	_____	_____
Parking	_____	_____	_____
Bus/mass transit/taxis	_____	_____	_____
Total Transportation Costs	$_____	_____	_____
Medical Expenses			
Insurance premium	_____	_____	_____
Prescriptions	_____	_____	_____
General health items	_____	_____	_____
Medical bills not covered by insurance (include deductible)	_____	_____	_____
Other_____	_____	_____	_____
Total Medical Expenses	$_____	_____	_____
Loan Payments			
Installment loans	_____	_____	_____
Credit card and interest	_____	_____	_____
Personal Loans	_____	_____	_____
Total Loan payments	$_____	_____	_____
Fixed Expenses			
Professional/union dues	_____	_____	_____
Professional services (legal and accounting)	_____	_____	_____
Business expenses not reimbursed	_____	_____	_____
Child care/babysitting	_____	_____	_____
Alimony/child support	_____	_____	_____
Total Fixed Expenses	$_____	_____	_____

	Present minus	New Budget =	Savings
*Club Memberships/Dues	$_____	_____	_____
*Religious Organization Dues	$_____	_____	_____
*Pet Expenses	$_____	_____	_____
Education			
College tuition/room & board	_____	_____	_____
*Private schools and lessons	_____	_____	_____
School supplies	_____	_____	_____
Professional improvement	_____	_____	_____
Other_____	_____	_____	_____
Total Education Costs	$_____	_____	_____
Entertainment			
*Sports/health clubs/activity	_____	_____	_____
*Reading material/subscriptions	_____	_____	_____
*Performances & Sports Events	_____	_____	_____
*Cable/satellite television	_____	_____	_____
*Video rentals	_____	_____	_____
*Other_____	_____	_____	_____
Total Entertainment Costs	$_____	_____	_____
*Cigarettes/liquor/luxury items	$_____	_____	_____
1. Subtotal Routine Living Expenses	$_____	_____	_____
Taxes			
Income tax	_____	_____	_____
Social security	_____	_____	_____

	Present	minus New Budget	= Savings
State Income tax	_____	_____	_____
Property tax	_____	_____	_____
Other_____	_____	_____	_____
2. Subtotal Taxes	$_____	_____	_____

Discretionary Expenses

*Vacations/trips	_____	_____	_____
*Charitable donations	_____	_____	_____
*Gifts	_____	_____	_____

Savings

Regular Savings	_____		
Retirement funds (IRA, Keogh, TSA)	_____		
College fund	_____		
Speculative (stocks, etc.)	_____		
Other savings	_____		
Total Savings	$_____ (**X**)		
Specific Investment items	$_____	_____	_____
Other_____	$_____	_____	_____
3. Subtotal Discretionary Expenses	$_____	_____	_____

B. Total Living Expenses: add Routine Living, Taxes & Discretionary Expenses (lines 1 + 2 + 3)	$_____	_____	_____ (**Y**)

Difference Between Income and Expenses
(Subtract Line B from Line A) $_____ (**Z**)

Total Monthly Savings (X + Y + Z) $_____

SAVING TIPS

To further increase your savings, you can apply the principles of planning, maximizing efficiency, and conserving. Some examples of how you can do this with regard to household expenses follow below:

Food and other consumables

✔ Eat at home more often
✔ Plan menus in advance
✔ Buy bulk foods with long shelf life
✔ Buy fruits and vegetables in season only
✔ Avoid processed, "junk," and "convenience" foods
✔ Save leftovers
✔ If you do not know how, learn to cook
✔ When possible buy directly from producers through farmer's markets and cooperatives

—Fill in the Following Lines With Your Own Ideas—

_____

_____

_____

_____

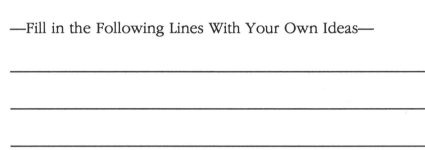

Household utilities

✔ Turn off unused appliances and lights
✔ Check the seal on your refrigerator to make sure no energy is leaking (the refrigerator uses more electricity than any other appliance in most American homes).
✔ Lower the heat or air conditioning at night and when no one is home
✔ Turn down the thermostat on your hot water heater
✔ When not actually using water turn it off (such as when brushing teeth or washing dishes)
✔ Water the lawn not the street
✔ Water at the cooler time of the day, not in the heat of the day
✔ Run the washer, dryer, or dishwasher with a full load

—Fill in With Your Own Ideas—

_____

_____

_____

_____

Transportation

✔ Walk or ride a bicycle whenever possible
✔ Cluster your errands
✔ Turn off the car engine when you stop for more than 30 seconds
✔ Drive a fuel efficient automobile if you have a choice
✔ Take public transportation whenever possible
✔ Do preventative maintenance on your car
✔ Vacation in the United States when the exchange rate is poor
✔ Plan travel well in advance to get maximum discounts

—Fill in with Your Own Ideas—

_____

_____

_____

_____

Other tips

✔ If you are relatively healthy, reduce your health insurance premium with a higher deductible
✔ Delay major purchases such as a house, automobile, large appliances, and furniture until after the depression begins and prices fall
✔ Ask your employer if you can take money that has previously been deducted for a pension plan in cash
✔ More tips will be included in the chapters on investments and lifestyle

—Fill in with Your Own Ideas—

_____

_____

_____

By filling in the above charts and establishing a personal budget with savings as the major priority, you can mitigate the impact of the coming depression. At first these changes may be uncomfortable, especially in contrast with our current lifestyle. The average U.S. citizen commands, in Btu (British Thermal Unit) equivalent, the services of 100 slaves.[12] This level of consumption has been fueled by easily available credit, a fairly stable job market, and a financial system that has been relatively free from catastrophe for fifty years. When the crash and subsequent depression hits with hurricane force, these three elements will be leveled to their roots, and everything will change.

Those who have lived through a depression are much more aware of the sacrifices and hardships that will have to be endured. They survived a time when money was not available and shake their heads sadly when observing the spending and consuming of the younger generation.

In our headlong rush towards acquisition, important values have been lost, most notably the wisdom of living within our means and giving the welfare of others as much importance as we give our own. American author Budd Schulberg writes at age 73, "This is a new nation with idealistic individuality contending with selfish individualism . . . individualism run rampant, with arrogant disregard for the views and welfare of our fellow men."[13]

As a generation and a nation, we need to return to a philosophy of saving and preparing for the inevitable rainy day. The soaring national debt is a testament to the mortgaging of our future and our children's future. This debt is rapidly coming due. Our society is so accustomed to its high standard of living that we, as a nation, are unwilling to take the actions necessary to prevent the coming economic disaster. However, as individuals we can prepare and begin to put ourselves and our loved ones in a position to avoid the worst impact. Each family can consider what its needs are today and what its needs are likely to be during the depression. Through planning, budgeting, and saving, we can get ready. By saving now, we can lessen our family's suffering.

The following chapter presents a plan showing where to invest the money you saved. This will insure the maximum protection, liquidity, and return on your hard saved dollars.

Endnotes

1. Harvard Economic Society, "General Economic Conditions in the United States," *The Review of Economic Statistics,* vol. XVII no. 1, January 15, 1935, p. 8.

2. Harvard Economic Society, "Review of the Year 1931," *The Review of Economic Statistics,* vol. XIV, no. 1, February 15, 1932, p. 20.

3. Studs Terkel, interview with Sidney Weinberg, *Hard Times* (New York: Pantheon Books), p. 94.

4. "Major Borrowing and Lending Trends in the U.S. Economy, 1981—85," *Federal Reserve Bulletin,* vol. 72, no. 8, August, 1986, p. 511.

5. Hugh Brogan, *The Longman History of the United States,* (New York: William Morrow and Company, 1985), pp. 531-534.

6. Paul Hawken, *The Next Economy,* (New York: Holt, Rinehart, and Winston, 1983), p. 52.

7. Robert S. McElvaine, *The Great Depression in America, 1929—1941,* (New York: Times Books, 1984), p. 137.

8. Harold Whitman Bradley, *The United States from 1865,* (New York: Charles Scribner and Sons, 1973), p. 283.

9. "1985 Annual Report, FDIC," Washington D.C., p. 70.

10. Richard Alm and Robert Morse, "The American Savings Slump — a Fluke or a Real Threat?," *U.S. News and World Report,* November 25, 1985, p. 64.

11. Lindley H. Clark, Jr., "Personal Saving Rate Heads for 40 Year Low," *The Wall Street Journal,* May 11, 1987, p. 1.

12. Hawken, p. 17.

13. Richard Reeves, quoting Budd Schulberg, *The Denver Post,* August 14, 1987, p. 35.

Chapter
6
Personal Investment Strategy

Having produced excess money over your daily needs, the next question is, "What do I do with it?" Normally, the answer is to invest it, to put this spare money to work for you. Economic conditions alter investment goals. With the coming of the depression, the most important goal of investing is the preserving of capital.

During depressions, values drop. For most investors, the most important goal will be to prevent their investment capital and assets from disappearing. Protection becomes much more important than the hope of future return. The days of easily making a killing on the market have ended. The long term economic growth necessary to increase the value of businesses and property holdings has vanished. The world economy has almost filled the entire volume it can occupy under the present system. Future growth will only come after economic shrinkage. To invest wisely then means to have your investment principal available when you need it most. During the coming economic upheaval, quick access to your investment capital may become essential.

The purpose of saving money is to have it available when needed. Money is best spent when it sustains or enhances life. Investments are normally defined as vehicles into which you place money so it will grow. Since investing is a form of spending, good investments are those which most efficiently use money as a resource.

People's needs vary. People with little spare money have very different financial priorities than those with surplus cash. For all, however, it is important to have a way to determine the right methods and places to put cash today where it will do you the most good.

Traditionally, investment vehicles involve some form of tangible property or paper promise of performance — known as a security. They can be further divided on the basis of whether or not they produce income over time.

These four categories of investment are shown on the following page:

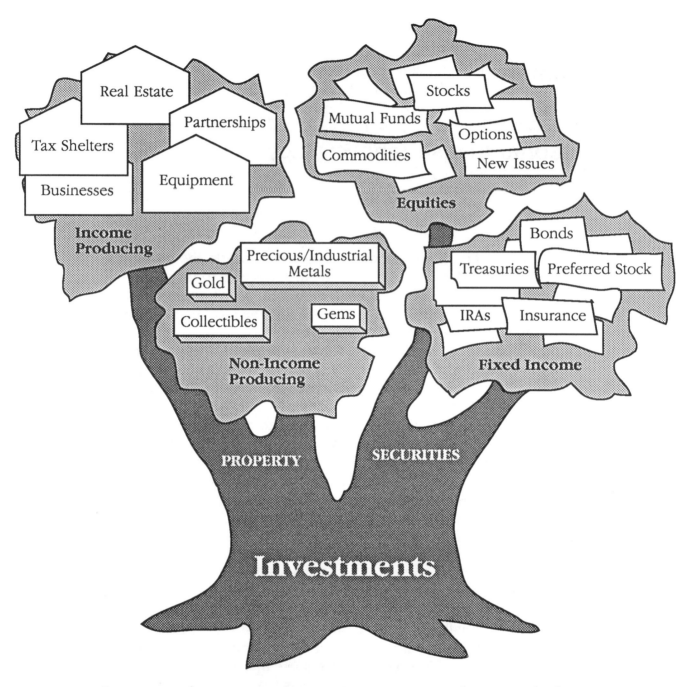

Investments have certain elements in common. To determine the best investments for the coming depression, it is necessary to identify their various elements and examine how they affect the choices you will make. These are:

1. Cost
2. Return — More money comes back
3. Risk — Danger of loss
4. Volatility — How fast and far values can change
5. Time — Length of investment period
6. Liquidity — Ability for investor to get invested funds.
7. Involvement — Amount of work in the investment

As we enter the depression, prices (values) drop and risk increases. This means investments that run fewer risks and carry less danger of losing value, are recommended. Goods, services, property and valuable objects all have lower prices. Consequently, those who need to see a return at any time during the coming depression are limited to investments that are guaranteed to show a return over the short term.

RETURN, RISK, AND LIQUIDITY

Expected return becomes meaningless when the original investment disappears. Even though stocks and bonds have yielded a return of between 14% and 17% during some economic downturns, it is important to measure the relative degree of safety. Liquidity also becomes more important. An investment that does not make money available when it is most needed, or one that does not allow the investor to withdraw the initial capital at the time of the greatest risk (panic) is the same as losing that money. This is not the purpose of investing.

TIMING IS CRITICAL

Risk can be managed, by some people, with timing and care. The financial burdens imposed on our economic system are going to strongly alter it very soon. For most people, the most critical investing step will involve the preservation of their assets.

Keeping your home or savings intact represents sound investing. Zero percent growth during a time of massive shrinkage represents a high true return on investment. In fact, money coming in during a time when other money and values disappear is much like having an increasing income — a desired result from investments.

Timing means investing in the right vehicle at the right time. If you can get a real return of 2% safely versus risking a 25% to 40% loss on a possible 10% return, which choice would you make? The answer depends on the individual, but there are times when returns, as measured against the risk, do not pay — no matter how high they are projected to be. This is one of those times.

CHOOSING AN INVESTMENT

In determining the type of investment category(ies) you will choose, it is important to assess the types of risk each category carries. Keep the following in mind:

1. The investment may lose so much value that it becomes impossible to sell. Examples would include new issues, stocks, real estate, art/collectibles.

2. Leveraged investments, during a time of economic shrinkage and falling markets, can force the investor to continually add money to the investment to cover margin losses. Eventually the investor may lose several times the original investment through negative leverage. While commodities, options, stocks and futures are normal representative examples of this type of risk, Americans have added home equity loans. If you borrow against the value of your home — and housing values fall in a depression — you may lose your home.

3. Inflation destroys some investment values, often lowering redemption prices below purchase prices. Inflation, after an initial bout as the government makes a final effort to prevent the depression, is unlikely to be a major factor. Normally this type of risk is limited to fixed income vehicles like Treasury, corporate and municipal bonds.

For most investors then, properties can be eliminated on the basis of risk, volatility, liquidity and the time it takes to get a return. With regard to securities, risk becomes highly critical. Although stocks and bonds can make money in recessions, for most people the stock market represents the unacceptable risk of huge losses from the market fall and the subsequent depression.

Present economic information shows great uncertainty for the future along with tremendous potential risks. Contrarians say this is the time to make the largest gains. They may be correct. However, the highest priority is to keep you and those closest to you intact during a time of extreme financial change. To make large investment profits at the beginning of a depression requires abilities and resources well beyond the means of most investors.

The stock market carries inordinate risk; other equities are equally or more dangerous. Property values will fall during the depression. This leaves the traditional refuge for downturn investing — fixed income, short term vehicles.

FIXED INCOME VEHICLES

One assumption is that our present form of government will survive in some recognizable form through the depression. At least at the beginning of the depression, U.S. government debt issues like Treasury bills and bonds will be safe. This means investing in the U.S. government will represent a form of guaranteed repayment. And that will make it popular with both American and foreign investors. The list below shows fixed income investments starting with the safest.

United States Savings Bonds
Always redeemable at par value, backed by the U.S. Treasury. In general, the safer the bond, the lower its interest return. Savings bonds suffer severe losses in times of inflation. *The Wall Street Journal* carries

daily quotations on U.S. savings bonds, Treasury certificates and agency obligations in a column called "Government, Agency and Miscellaneous Securities."

United States Treasury Bills

Three, six, and twelve months in length. Backed by the full faith and credit of U.S. government, these T- Bills are very liquid interest bearing cash. Due to the extreme uncertainty of our economy, investing in the shorter term notes is highly recommended. Six months from now, conditions may be very different. T-Bills require a minimum investment of $10,000. To buy T-bills directly, go to a U.S. Federal Reserve bank or branch, or send a letter to:

Bureau of Public Debt
Treasury Department
Washington, D.C. 20220

You can ask for information on how to buy, or send them a check for $10,000 and ask to enter a "non-competitive bid." You will be charged the average auction price of the bills and sent a check for the remainder by return mail, in effect buying your T-bills at a discount and receiving your interest in advance. The Treasury will send your T-bills by registered mail.

United States Treasury Notes

Longer term than T-Bills, these notes range from one to seven years and pay slightly higher interest. Their risk of erosion through inflation becomes much greater. Their longer term leaves you much more exposed to risk if you try to sell them in the open marketplace before they mature.

In order to lock in a good rate of return in a falling market, T-notes are a worthwhile risk. Usually they are available to the smaller investor for $1,000, but when the government worries about the flow of money from savings institutions into T-notes, it will raise the minimum purchase price to $10,000. Assuming the government can keep its financial commitments for the first three years of the depression, these notes are an acceptable risk. Any investment longer than three years in non-government backed vehicles carries a dangerous level of risk.

United States Treasury Bonds

With maturities running up to 25 years, these are the longest term government obligations of all. The market sees these bonds as losing value due to inflation compounded over time. One result is that the U.S. national debt is constantly becoming shorter in overall length. Do not invest here.

United States Government Agency Obligations

Federal agencies such as Government National Mortgage Association (Ginnie Mae) and the Federal Home Loan Mortgage Corporation (Freddie Mac) sell their own obligations, with maturities ranging from one month to 25 years. Some are backed by the government, others by the agency only. None have ever defaulted. In the event of a funding squeeze brought on by the economy, the government would allow an agency to fail first. Due to their slightly lower safety, they usually pay 0.3 % more on short term or 0.5% more interest on long term obligations than the Treasury. It is important to note that federal agencies are exempt from the reporting requirements of the S.E.C. Without such exemptions, many buyers would not have bought New York City bonds before their collapse in 1975.

Life insurance

Single premium whole life policies and some of the better universal life policies offer better long term returns to the investor than Treasuries. Buying life insurance allows the investor to participate in the higher yielding bonds with a diverse pool of Treasuries and corporate bonds with professional managers buying and selling at the theoretically correct time. Since they must be able to pay large claims at once, insurance companies usually follow a conservative investment method. Investing habits vary, but usually companies invest in a portfolio of Treasury bills, notes, and every type of bond. Normally, less than ten percent of an insurance company's investment portfolio is invested in stocks or real estate. Often they are big buyers of federal obligations.

Policies designed to meet the needs of the 30's overcharged life insurance policyholders until the early 80's. Current plans benefit from large company reserves filled with excess money for nearly 40 years since the last depression. Consequently, insurance money is backed by reserves several times as high as the federal backing on banks. State regulations normally require insurance companies to have additional insurance companies backing each insurance policy. During the Great Depression, over four thousand banks failed but less than 5% of the insurance companies had to close.

Modern life insurance policies offer large build-up and low charges. Some allow the owner to direct the company on which type of income vehicles to invest the policy's cash. Insurance earnings are tax deferred, allowing their annual income to be reinvested untaxed. This means that, over 20 years, insurance policies would return 50% more than the same investments held outside the policy. Most of the better policies have loan provisions that will loan out the principal at 0 to 2% net interest. Avoid policies charging more.

Insurance, to truly show a return, must be held for a minimum of five to seven years. Single premium whole life, with no loads or charges, will show an immediate return, but has surrender charges running from five to seven years. Under current law it is possible to pull a tax free annual income from these policies. All the good recent insurance policies guarantee a minimum of 4% to 6% per year. In a time of deflation and disappearing money, this 4% growth rate would seem like a windfall. It is important to note, however, that in times of emergency, insurance companies may take up to six months before sending out checks to policyholders. Check out all the minimum and maximum guarantees and charges. Some companies offer wire transfers or checking against policy values. Choose your policy carefully, and it can make you comfortable for as long as any vehicle presently available. At all times, insurance returns match or beat the cost of living indices.

The insurance industry is financially rated by an independent rating company, A. M. Best. You can find *Best's Review* in some public libraries, or go to the state division of insurance, insurance brokers or the companies themselves for the Best Rating. By carefully reading the reviews, you will have some idea of the financial fitness of the company and how they invest. Any A or A+ Best rated company that survived the last depression should stand a pretty good chance of surviving the next. To make sure the company you use is safe you can send $5 for their companies-to-watch list to:

Insurance Forum
P.O. Box 245
Ellettsville, IN 47429

It lists all insurance companies that have required regulatory attention in any of the last three years. If your company is on the list, move to a Best rated A or A+ company that is not on the list.

Credit unions

Credit unions, unlike banks, are owned by their members. Credit union accounts pay interest on deposits and charge lower fees on loans. Interest on deposits is paid to the depositors as dividends. Credit unions are backed by the National Credit Union Administration Share Insurance Fund (NCUASIF). This fund is backed between a level of 1.0% and 1.3% of every dollar on deposit. NCUASIF funding totals over 1.3% are re-paid to the overcharged credit unions, which returns this money to its members. Within the past few years, many credit unions have been offering their own version of money market funds.

Credit unions make consumer loans, not commercial loans like banks. These loans are very safe as they are based on an often personal bond between credit union members and their credit union. Even people going bankrupt frequently repay the credit union where they might not repay a bank. One result is that credit unions have fewer problem loans for smaller amounts. During the Great Depression of the 30's, no credit union failed. If your place of employment offers a credit union, join it. If not, you and your co-workers can together join a local credit union. Call any credit union to find out how to do this. This is a good place to hold money during the next two years.

Savings accounts

Savings accounts are pledged to return all money deposited, and most are backed by the Federal Depositors Insurance Corporation (FDIC) or the Federal Savings and Loan Insurance Corporation (FSLIC).

This backing is constantly dwindling and being subsequently replenished by the federal government. During 1987, over 200 banks failed, yet most depositors got their money within two weeks. During a depression or long term recession, many more banks may fail in a shorter time period, severely taxing federal efforts to keep the system solvent. If your bank fails during the depression, the government will attempt to meet its FDIC obligations. However, it may take several weeks or months before this money is dispatched to you, and the tremendous demand on an underfunded FDIC system may lead to settling for cents on the dollar.

Before investing in banks or savings and loans, check the health of your savings institution. A variety of options for doing this are listed below:

1. You can get the current financial statement of any bank by asking for it.

2. Banks and Savings and Loans are required to publish a quarterly summary of their activities in local newspapers.

3. For financial statements on a variety of banks you can contact:

The U.S. Office of Economic and Policy Research
1120 Connecticut Ave. NW, Washington, D.C. 20036
(202) 663-5130

For Savings and Loans contact:

The Federal Home Loan Board
P.O. Box 176, Topeka, Kansas 66601
(913) 233-0507

4. Commercial firms that will give you more detailed information on financial institutions for a fee include the following:

For banks and Savings and Loans:

P.J. Holt Company
290 Post Rd. West
Westport, Connecticut 06880
(800) 289-8100

For banks:

Veribank
P.O. Box 2963
Woburn, Massachussets 01888
(617) 245-8370

Shehunoff and Company, Inc.
1 Texas Center
Austin, Texas 78704
(512) 472-2244

Avoid banks with more than 1% non-performing loans or over 1% of their loans written off the books as a loss. They are having problems with their investment portfolios that may lead to their closing.

Money market accounts
These bank accounts are backed by FDIC and FSLIC. The investor can earn rates competitive with the market and 90 day Treasury Bills while remaining totally liquid. This possibly is one of the best short term places to wait until a future economic course is clearly indicated. Be sure to check the financial health of *any* institution where you invest a substantial amount of money.

Until 1982, money market accounts could only be bought through stock brokerage firms. Now banks are allowed to sell money market accounts. This is a good way to get the safety and return of Treasury Bills without the complication of buying them. Money market accounts are backed by the FDIC with its attendant virtues and risks.

Bank certificates of deposit
These are short term certificates of obligations by a bank to repay. Certificates are purchased for specific periods ranging from 30 days to several years. They are not as liquid as the various savings accounts, but their federal backing is the same. The larger floating rate CD's allow investors to readjust their interest rate or leave. Typically, they pay 1% over Treasury bill rate and are redeemable on a regular basis. Recently,

banks have started offering flexible and increasing rate CD's to smaller investors.

Government money market mutual funds

These funds hold short term government paper at market rates of interest. Their holdings usually include some mixture of U.S. Treasury bills, with an average maturity running between 20 and 90 days. The notes are backed by the U.S. Treasury.

The investor's account is insured by the Securities Investors Protection Corporation (SIPC). SIPC is a private corporation with a one-half billion dollar private line of credit and a further one billion line with the U.S. Treasury. Individual accounts are covered for up to $100,000 in cash, or a total of $500,000 in cash and securities. However, if the brokerage house goes broke, your money market account — whether federal or otherwise — will only have the number of shares replaced. Any gain or loss in individual share value is your concern, not SIPC's.

Government money market mutual funds represent an acceptable level of risk while returning a slightly higher yield than T-Bills. The money in these funds is very liquid. They offer relative safety and liquidity with a higher rate return. For many small investors they are a good short term place for money. These funds — like all investments — must be watched very closely. Look for them in your newspaper under the "Donohue Bond Watcher."

The following investment vehicles are too common to be ignored, but are not recommended:

Banker's acceptance

These are certificates issued by a corporation, accepted by a bank and backed by the goods involved in the deal. Their normal time runs between 30 and 90 days to maturity. Although none has ever defaulted, they pay between one-half and one point over Treasury bond yields. Normally they run for very short terms and require at least $100,000 to buy.

Money market mutual funds

Money market mutual funds differ from government money market mutual funds by including large non- government CD's, banker's acceptances, commercial paper and other short term deposit securities. These mutual funds offer higher risk than the government funds. They are not backed by any government agency and offer an unacceptable risk.

Municipal bonds

Municipal bonds are an obligation by any state, county, city, water district, school district, sanitation district, municipality or any other governmental entity. These are far less safe than federal obligations, because these municipalities cannot print their own money. As the United States and much of the world runs on deficit economies, so do most states, cities and other governing bodies.

If cash runs short, the municipality may decide to pay its workers before paying their creditors. New York City did this in 1975 with apparent federal backing. During the last depression, 15% of the municipal bonds in this country failed. During the next depression, many municipalities may be unable to meet their bond obligations.

New York City set a precedent regarding the actual meaning of the promise of return on municipal bonds. The day before New York City defaulted on its bonds, they were rated AA. Recent federal tax rulings target municipal bonds' tax free status for corporate holders. This means that 30% of the municipal bond market could disappear over the next few years without a depression. The biggest losers would be cities using bonds for building or cash needs.

If inflation reappears at any time, bonds will rapidly lose their spending value versus the dollar. If interest rates drop, many bonds have a "call" feature allowing the municipality to call the bond in and replace it with one paying less interest. All in all, they are too risky and have poor liquidity. Stay away from municipal bonds.

Corporate bonds

Bonds normally run five to seven years. The buyer loans money to a corporation, which backs it with its strength and stability. Bonds provide more income than money market funds, CD's and other short term vehicles. During recessions, bonds tend to make good returns. However, the coming depression will destroy many businesses rendering their bonds worthless. The length of the bond terms combined with their low liquidity in recessions, make them too risky for most investors also.

With business debt levels over two times as high as U.S. Treasury debt, corporate bonds are somewhat more risky. Bond prices are based on the credit rating of the borrower. Corporate bonds are backed only by the corporation issuing them, some of which will fail during the coming depression. Many bonds have a call provision allowing the issuing company to call them in and replace them with lower yielding bonds. Corporate bonds are not recommended at this time despite their track record in the 30's.

Convertible bonds

Convertible bonds allow the holder to receive regular interest and can convert at the bondholder's request into common stock. This means company debt is convertible into equity. Do not buy them now.

Preferred stock

Like bonds, these too return fixed interest, but unlike bonds have no maturity date. Should a corporation have to settle its assets, preferred stocks rank lower than bonds on the obligation train but higher than common stock.

In a normal recession, many experts recommend bonds as a safe hedge. But this is not a normal recession coming; it is a world wide depression. Many areas of our world economy are so heavily in debt that when one part falls, all will fall.

Where do you hide from this massive debt contraction? Not in long term debt. Stay with the U.S. government in some form. This means that you may make less money in the current investment climate for a brief period of time. But this short term loss will be followed by the preservation of values in your investment, as investors world wide look to the U.S. government for safety and refuge as their values fall in other, riskier, investments.

EQUITIES — THE STOCK MARKET

The more risk, the more important it becomes to invest only what you can afford to lose. This is especially true in highly speculative investments like the stock, commodities and futures markets. Since the coming depression will also remove many sources of income, you should invest only what you do not need over the next five years. If you cannot afford to lose money, do not invest. Keep it close and watch the news.

Timing (patience) is everything. The time to buy stocks is after the market has fallen to its true bottom. Stocks were considered a bargain in the last quarter of 1929. Buyers who bought at the pit after the first major drop in the 1929, before the three year price slide into 1933, did not break even again until 1946.[1] Between 1929 and 1932, common stocks lost over 21 percent of their pre-fall value every year for four years. Those who waited three years for the market drop to fully run its course before buying made over fifty percent profit in 1934, while the earlier buyers were still trying to break even.

Based on return, stocks were not a good investment after the stock market crash in 1929. The same stocks showed a 33 percent annual growth rate when bought after the market low in 1932. What this means for most of you is: *Wait, wait, wait.* Let the market fall before buying into it.

Before the predicted crash and depression, there may well be many rises in stock prices. You can also count on a nerve wracking volatility and wild stock price swings. The effect of these swings can slice up the small investor, who can even lose money in the face of upward market trends by failing to time moves correctly. An illustration of why you should wait is presented below:

1. Let us pretend the Dow is at a hypothetical 2000 and is expected to rise as high as 3000, then fall down possibly as low as 1000.

2. Two thousand dollars is spent buying one share of each of the Dow 30 (the thirty stocks that make up the Dow Jones Industrial Average on the New York Stock Exchange). Brokerage fees are a moderate $50

Return on $2000 Investment if Dow Goes to 3000

	Sale Price	$2,400	
minus	Purchase Price	-2,000	
equals	Gross Profit	= 400	
minus	Brokerage Fees	-110	
minus	Federal Taxes	-60 (at 15%) or 112 (at 28%)	
equals	Net Profit	$230	or 178

---

from a discount broker. If the Dow reaches 3000 and you have the luck or skill to sell within 20% of the top (where most people buy, not sell), then your stock is worth $2400. (.80 X 3000 = 3200). An identical brokerage commission percentage would cost $60. The result would look like the chart above. A $230 profit represents a return of 11.5%. $178 brings a return of 8.9%. Both returns, if gotten within one or two months are wonderful, but the $2000 risk at this time is just too high.

Return on $2,000 if Dow Drops From 2,000 to 1,000

	Price at Sale	$900	
minus	Purchase Price	-2,000	
equals	Gross Loss	(1,100)	loss
minus	Brokerage Fees (basic)	-100	
equals	Net Loss	(1,200)	loss

How high? What happens if the market precipitously drops to 1000 and you manage to get out within 25% of the bottom? Bid prices (highest market buying price) might be well below what the Dow called for. An example of this is shown above. A long-term major stock market loss is very hard on your nerves — and your family's. This loss could occur over a period from six months to three years. Prices could remain depressed at these levels for years. During this time, your investment would not have increased any type of wealth, happiness, or helped sustain life.

Greed makes people buy at the top; fear makes them sell at the bottom. In a rapidly shifting and ultimately falling market, these two factors will ensure huge losses to the majority of investors.

Investment planning

Every investor should develop an investment plan and set goals. The goals will tell you how much money you need to make or have. The plan will tell you how to get there. Presently, the recommended investment goal is to keep your money intact for the next few years, despite the temptation to buy. Remember the free fall panic of October, 1987 on the New York and 22 other major stock exchanges around the world. The emotional euphoria from hitting the stock market rise does not last nearly as long as the sadness produced by getting caught in the crash.

No matter what information is offered, some people wish to speculate. In order to speculate during the coming dramatic changes, you need to develop specialized financial knowledge or find a good financial planner or market timer with a track record and outlook that matches your needs. This means know what rise or drop you are willing to sell your investment at — before you buy — and stick to these numbers no matter what happens in the market. When you buy, put in a stop loss order telling the broker the price at which you will sell. Then sit back and wait. And hope. This course is not recommended.

For more information on choosing funds, the *Hulbert Financial Digest* rates stocks, mutual funds, commodities and other types of vehicles. They can be reached at 1-800-443-0100. Market investment strategies vary. To find one look in *Money, Barrons,* or *The Wall Street Journal* for successful managers with good track records during recent recessions or crashes.

Like bringing a sailboat into a rocky lee shore with huge waves and shifting winds, gather information carefully, then pick your moment. Knowledge and patience have great value to investors, much more than hasty choices. Do not look for quick answers; look for good answers.

Diversification

Diversifying in different bills, bonds and funds is important in order to lower risk. Buy government money market mutual funds. Typically, to invest requires $1000 to $2000. Look for the Donohue Fund yields in your newspaper, and get the prospectus on funds that interest you.

Traditional investment advice is to diversify investment money among four groups: Cash, fixed-income securities, growth stocks and non-liquid assets. For example, individuals would invest 25-40% in stocks and divide the rest among long term bonds, Treasury bills and notes.

This would be a very reasonable approach if the risks facing our economy were not so huge. Considering the severity and rapidity of the coming economic changes, prudence dictates that anyone who must have access to all their money for financial survival in the next five years should keep it in cash or the short term vehicles recommended earlier.

Stock Mutual Funds have been highly rated as a means of diversification. All types of different funds proliferated before the crash of 1929, and over 500 mutual funds are available today. Spreading risks did not prevent mutual funds from taking a 16.4% average beating in the October, 1987 crash. *Money* tracked the performance of the top ten mutual funds for 1987 through the end of September, comparing their return for the first nine months of the year with October returns. The mutual funds took losses. After the crash in October, many fund managers moved into more cash and away from the market.

None of these fund's managers give any guarantees. Professional fund managers control 70% of the money in the New York Stock Exchange. Over time the fund managers will determine the market average by their performance. If the market is falling and you invest with them, you will see these falls in the form of dwindling returns on your shares. Professional managers, much like gamblers, always have back-up funds and plans. Among the vehicles they use to protect against devastating losses are options and stock index futures. To go into the present market without a backup is far too dangerous for most individuals.

Commodities Futures and Options are speculative vehicles designed to leverage money on the stock or commodities (i.e. gold, soybeans, orange juice) markets. These investments usually make more commissions for the broker than profits for anyone else. 75% of all options expire worthless. 10% of the commodities players make 90% of the money. Typically, the investor puts up 3% to 10% of the commodity purchase price, leaving her or him vulnerable to losing even more money if the market price goes the other way. For the new investor both of these are out of the question.

Options make sense as portfolio insurance. Buying *Puts* (the right to sell later at a lower price) is one "apparent" way to lock in a profit with your losses. When sold in large amounts over a short period of time, Puts can cause or contribute to a stock market crash. According to the Brady Commission report on the market crash of 1987, option sales by large fund managers and program trading drove prices down on the New York and Chicago exchanges, causing the crash. When the options were most needed as portfolio insurance, the sell orders became impossible to fill as sellers vastly outnumbered buyers. This made the most volatile investment totally illiquid at a crucial time, which led to huge losses. Perhaps the beginning of the coming depression will be heralded by the disappearance of liquidity on the options or commodities market.

Selling short is the borrowing and selling of stock you don't own based on the expectation of falling prices. For example, by calling a broker and asking him or her to sell stock and then buying it back on the market place at a lower price later, you are selling short. While the stock is sold you have to pay the stock broker a relatively high rate of interest until you have bought an equal number of shares to replace them in the broker's portfolio. This strategy works best in a rapidly falling market. A slow fall or an increase in stock prices can spell disaster for the unwary investor. Selling short is an extremely risky proposition.

Drops of 508 points were unthinkable in 1986; 769 points in four days would have seemed totally unlikely. But the market is *the* Leading Indicator of the economy. It fell. It will fall again. If it continues flat or rises and stays higher for over a year, just remember it will fall. What goes up must come down. Sit back and let the market happen.

INCOME PRODUCING PROPERTY AND BUSINESSES

Income producing property is a traditional big loser in a deflationary recession or depression. Houses and property lost forty percent of their collective value during the Depression of the 30's.

Income producing properties and business ventures normally appreciate over time. The investor owns a tangible property from which both value appreciation and income — in the form of a positive cash flow — are expected. Values drop during depressions. From 1929 to 1932 the DJIA lost over three quarters of its value. As businesses lose value, they lower prices and concentrate on staying in business. This type of activity does not generate profits for the owners, but may produce losses.

If you own or operate a business, take the following steps:

1. Lower your Accounts Receivable backlog today.

2. Take steps to eliminate unnecessary debt at once.

3. For businesses, renegotiate your lease. If your lease is expiring, renew it on a short term lease. This will pay even if you have to offer your landlord more money to do so. Before the crash in 1929, the president of A&P Foods took this unusual step. As a result, when rent prices fell over 40% during the Great Depression of the 30's, his chain was not burdened with high rents.

4. If you have been thinking of selling, do it now. Unless your business is recession/depression proof, you are unlikely to ever get a higher price for it.

Owning your own home

More Americans save by investing in their homes than any other means. During the mid-1980's, many took out home equity loans to buy consumer goods. The principle of mortgaging homes to the hilt is based on the illusion of continually escalating real estate prices.

In a deflationary depression homes lose value. When home values fall holders of home equity loans may be in the unenviable position of having to pay interest on loans that are higher than the value of their house. These payments will be difficult, if not impossible, to cover during the depression. Failure to cover the loan payment can lead to the loss of your home. Take steps to prevent this:

1. Anyone with a fixed real estate or home equity loan should look at refinancing with a variable rate mortgage — unless you have a very old loan at interest rates below 7%. During the Depression of the 1930's home mortgage loans were routinely available at 2%.

2. If you do not like your house, or intend to move, sell now — while the market still exists. If you do sell, consider renting until after the depression hits and prices and interest rates are much lower. A depressed market means that sellers will have to be much more flexible on price. During the depression, these prices will fall further.

3. Negotiate a real estate brokerage commission lower than the standard 7%. Although many realtors refuse to lower their commission, some will. In the listing agreement, include a clause stating that the realtor's fee will be lowered two to two and a half points if they do not have to split their fee with another realtor.

Income producing real estate

It is already apparent that long term investments are extremely risky. Although real estate will eventually increase in value, it may take more than ten years to see prices recover to the point they were at before their fall.

Owning real estate beyond your own home is very risky at this time. When jobs and money are scarce, income producing real estate may lose income and will lose value. Real estate is probably the most highly leveraged investment with the exception of commodities futures. Properties with equity loans on them will cripple the owner with high payments during a time of minimal cash availability. Commercial property and residential rental property should generate strong negative cash flows during the depression, resulting in widespread foreclosures.

GOLD AND NON-INCOME-PRODUCING PROPERTY

For the past four thousand years, during periods of severe economic trial, gold has ranked from being the best choice to the only choice. Traditionally gold holds value very well during periods of inflation and does poorly in recessions. If the depression is strong enough to cause the dollar to collapse, a small amount of gold will prove worthwhile. As a speculation it may not be profitable, but for security in a tough world it is unbeatable.

Gold holds value over time. An ounce of gold would have bought a very good man's dress suit after the Revolutionary War, the Civil War, World War I and would do so today. There is always a market for gold. It is sold through brokers and on exchanges all over the world. Most of the sales are in the form of coins and small bars to small purchasers. In times of fear, people buy gold. In many of the developing countries gold is trusted far more than banks.

Precious metals and diamonds

When recessions hit, values drop. When business slows the value of silver and platinum and other industrial metals drops. The only way these items gain value is if the underlying currency or government of the country is in danger of failing. The depression will exert extreme pressure on the government and the dollar. Perhaps both will emerge on the other side. If you feel the dollar will disappear, these investments will pay off during the next five to seven years.

Diamonds are tightly controlled by cartels, and their prices may not reflect availability. As a hedge against the depression, they are much less preferable than gold.

During normal times, most investors lose money on their investments. These are not normal times; money will become scarce, and lost money will be impossible for most people to replace. Investors need to stay risk free and liquid until the investment climate improves. This means stay close to the U.S. government, with government money market mutual funds and Treasury bills or notes. For those who can afford it, buy a little gold. Stay away from real estate, business ventures, and the stock market. The time for them will come later.

Endnotes

1. Jane Bryant Quinn, *Newsweek*, November 2, 1987, p. 39

Chapter

7

Earning a Living During the Depression

In the depression one-third of American workers will lose their jobs at one time or another. Every field will be affected. When having a job means a roof over one's head and regular meals, versus life on the streets, secure, meaningful employment becomes critical.

During a time of decreasing jobs and money, the most valued workers will be the ones most likely to work. The coming depression, like the last, will be a time when professional workers are the most valued. During the 30's engineers, technicians, draftsmen and scientists commanded relatively high salaries in somewhat more secure jobs than blue collar workers. The decade saw the wide introduction of synthetic fibers, all metal cars and aircraft, electricity, radios and labor saving appliances.

This chapter will show the major job trends underway in the work place, demonstrate how they will affect workers, address major fields of employment in the depression, and provide a structure for determining personal options in the light of this information.

CHANGES IN THE WORK PLACE

Presently, widespread technological changes are taking place in business and manufacturing. World wide telecommunications, computerization and automation are changing the way business is transacted. Lasers, databases and fiber optics vastly alter the amount and precision of information that can be used in making and selling virtually every product and service.

One result of these inventions is rapid and dramatic change. The current long term expectation for the world economy is for foreign and American businesses to use far more robots and computers in the increasingly competitive struggle for markets. The oncoming depression will slow this trend, but not reverse it.

A survey of employers by researchers from the Massachusetts Institute of Technology, as part of an eleven year study, found that America created over 7 million new jobs during the 1980's. Over eighty percent of these jobs were created in small companies with between one and ten employees.

To work, and hold secure valued work in a time of great changes, requires the ability to be flexible in adapting to change. The days of holding a steady manufacturing job, with little alteration in education or job skills, are over. Good precise work requires higher education and job skills wielded by workers who can change functions and job descriptions without major retraining.

Factory workers will be cross-trained to handle several different functions in manufacturing plants. They will work alone running computers operating basic machinery. Office workers individually will process more information, computers and electronic office equipment than was previously handled by several workers.

Because it is easier to develop new equipment than good people to operate and maintain it, the demand for workers qualified to do this will grow. The strength of this trend has not been widely perceived by the American public. As a result, highly skilled personnel are in short supply while former factory workers are unemployed. Within two years, this information will be generally known. It is best to get the jump on this trend now.

The U.S. Bureau of Labor Statistics claims the ten fastest growing jobs are low-end service jobs. None involve high technology. The positions include cashiers, registered nurses, janitors, truck drivers, waitresses and waiters and nursing aides. All of these jobs are in the service sector, paying on average 11% less than factory work. Most of these positions offer part time work — primarily to women. They pay 60% less than the top ten jobs in the service sector. After adjusting hourly wages for inflation, it is apparent that this work pays lower real wages than it did ten years ago. Competition for these jobs will be fierce during the depression, but they will barely feed a family and offer little or no security.

Between 1980 and 1987 the Fortune 500 companies lost three million jobs in the United States. During this same period, overseas manufacturing investment by major U.S. companies grew sixteen times as large. Although the domestic balance of trade deficit is the worst in American history, if one adds the U.S. exports to the exports of foreign subsidiaries of U.S. companies, one finds that U.S. companies still retain the same basic share of the world export market. It is just that their jobs are now in foreign countries.

The U.S. auto industry consumes a large percentage of domestic rubber, glass, and plastics output, half our steel production, and provides work for several hundred thousand subcontractors. As a result of foreign competition, 500,000 jobs disappeared in Michigan — the home of the American automobile industry — between 1978 and 1982. Three-fifths of these jobs were replaced with lower paying service jobs. Two-fifths of these jobs were never replaced. Many of the people who held those jobs — and their families — are homeless today.

DECLINING FIELDS IN THE DEPRESSION

Many basic industries and manufacturing concerns, long a part of the American economy, have been in depression for up to ten years. Others slowly slide down the slippery road of decline as worsening economic conditions catch them. Several sectors of the U.S. economy will decline regardless of the coming depression. Others will decline as a direct result of the depression. Some of these declining sectors include:

Automobile and heavy industry

Our economy relies on automobile production for a manufacturing base; however, with increased productivity and foreign manufacturing, there is now an over-capacity of several million cars over the market size. The auto industry has been laying off workers and will continue to lay off more. The depression will greatly accelerate this process. Most of those laid off will never work in their factories again.

As these people are laid off, factories will shut down. Recent layoffs of auto workers in Detroit have been followed by the increasing use of robot manufacturing of automobiles both in the United States and Japan. In the early 1980's, the president of General Motors said that between then and 1987, 90% of all the company's capital investment would be in robots. This holds true in the textile, glass, steel and rubber industries. It does not bode well for most American workers in basic industry.

Construction

Building requires buyers, and buyers require money and markets. Until falling costs match the downward flow of real estate values, construction industry employment will plummet. It will take several years for the economy to recover the vigor to promote growth in the form of new construction. New housing starts will continue to drop.

Financial and professional services

Employment of bankers, stock brokers, real estate agents and most financial consultants will plunge with the money supply. Marketing and advertising service workers, insurance agents, accountants, lawyers, and many other professional workers will see their work dwindle with the economy. Only the most talented will continue to work as the shake-out in the financial and professional service sector continues.

Office workers

The depression will erode the security of office workers and middle managers already weakened by office automation. Secretaries and low level decision makers will be replaced by fewer employees, who use computers to process and report information. These people will make more of their own decisions. Executives will learn to use office computers instead of relying on others to report to them. They will write their own reports instead of relying on a typist to do so. Those who are unable to use this technology will be replaced when companies start cutting back on staff.

Retail sales

As fewer people work and spend money, retail sales will drop. Even though most people will continue working during the earlier parts of the depression, high unemployment and consumer anxiety will cut deeply into retail sales. Consumer, luxury and frivolous goods will remain on store shelves. With lower sales, the need for sales people falls. This cut will reach into the light manufacturing companies making these products. Restaurants, tourism and related industries will sag.

Agriculture

The ongoing depression in agriculture will continue. Family farming declines as America consolidates its farms into large agribusinesses. Since these huge single crop farms depend more on the uninterrupted flow of energy, goods, services and workers, delays and hitches caused by the depression may impede the nation's food supply. The Bureau of Labor Statistics predicts that 3% of the nation's workers — the same percentage as today — will be employed in agriculture by the year 2020.

Armed forces

Defense spending and the military will decline as the government is forced by economic necessity to put more money into the economy and human services. Military spending provides little economic return. The debate between spending on guns or butter will at least temporarily be forced to tilt heavily in favor of butter.

Mining and utilities

These areas will decline as we buy fewer goods; manufacturing orders drop; and raw material and power needs slow. Although America was electrified during the Depression of the 30's, during the coming depression the government will gain nothing by subsidizing electricity use. Utilities, especially nuclear based utilities with their huge capital costs, will face tremendous financial pressures. America's miners will be the last workers re-hired at the end of the depression.

STEADY AND GROWING FIELDS

In order to predict secure fields, it is important to look at the information we already have. Labor intensive and non-essential industries are vulnerable to both the long term technological trend and the depression. The days of full employment and forty hour work weeks are rapidly ending. The time for one-job thirty-year careers has passed. The shift is to service jobs, especially those in government, health, and data processing.

Assuming our system of government and way of life survive the coming depression, the following industries should show level or growing employment during the depression:

Government workers

When things get bad, most people look to the government for help. As a result, government will grow during the depression. The increase in the number of aid and entitlement programs as more Americans suffer will be an indicator of how many more people will be employed by the government. This number — at least for the short term — should increase by several hundred thousand nationwide. The ability to understand potentially very complex programs and easily utilize computers will require moderate to high levels of technical skills.

Scientists and engineers

Traditionally, American companies use periods of depression to improve manufacturing processes. Falling steel and automobile sales in America, due to technologically inferior products and a lack of planning, led these and other companies to lay off millions of workers during the late 1970's. Since labor is a major component of cost, when costs must be cut, industry's answer is to reduce the work force. Historically, productivity rises during depressions in the United States as companies use economic expedience as the means to circumvent union contracts, lay off workers, and install labor saving machinery.

To compete in our economic system on the basis of quality means that automating manufacturing and information sharing capacity is inevitable. The trend is to reduce manufacturing costs by using less people, employing robots and generally making the entire manufacturing phase automatic.

The people who invent, design, sell, install, run and maintain the resulting technologies will be highly valued workers until American businesses are far more automated. Scientists and engineers will form the basis of this growth area. Technicians who can run these systems and learn new ones as they are installed will be employable for several decades.

Social service workers

Social work is a growth industry in depressions. Social workers were needed to administer New Deal social programs during the last depression. Federal spending for social programs should increase during the coming depression. However, those employed in private agencies are likely to see severe cutbacks due to a lack of charitable funding once the nation's money supply shrinks. Their only hope of staying employed in their current positions is if the government contracts for relief work with private agencies as well as public agencies.

Public works

During the Depression of the 1930's a barrage of government agencies worked on projects as varied as building dams and roads, writing plays and cutting trails in national forests and parks. The infrastructure of modern America was conceived in the 1950's and built in the 1960's. Our roads, highways, transit, water and sewer systems need work. Hundreds of billions of dollars will be spent on this. These jobs will require operating engineers, heavy equipment operators, and some less skilled laborers.

Pollution control

Acid rain is destroying forests all over the world. Millions of steel drums holding highly poisonous chemicals have passed thirty years in age and will start leaking horribly toxic materials into the ground and water supplies. Increasingly sophisticated scientific measuring devices can detect and measure these chemicals in our water supply. The growing data linking these chemicals and disease or death will lead to increasing public fear and anger. To quell this anger, companies and governments will be compelled to spend billions of dollars hiring several hundred thousand workers to decontaminate and move the messes to some other place. If the human race is to survive, pollution control will become a growth industry over the next 25 years.

Biologists, genetic engineers, medical workers

The ability to produce new species of microorganisms, plants and animals will strongly alter the shape of this society. Gasahol, AIDS vaccine development, new species of medicine producing and waste reducing bacteria and enhanced crop species result from biological and genetic research. Most of the actual work on these products will come from technicians operating sophisticated laboratory and precision production equipment. As these biotechnical inventions are increasingly brought to market, more biologists will be needed to continue this trend or fight the effects of some of the less successful inventions. Escalating world wide pollution will require major damage control in the next ten years. Biologists and ecologists may be in short supply at a critical time, especially with the current trend among U.S. college students away from engineering and biological sciences.

The spread of new infectious diseases such as AIDS, an aging American populace, and the ability to employ new technologies to, hopefully, enhance lives, will cause the trend of increasing expenditures on medicine to continue. Population growth will lead to increasing numbers of people being treated for diseases and injuries due to over-population, pollution and war. Medical workers will make less in the future, as this society's ability to pay for necessary services decreases, but their jobs will be fairly secure.

Teachers

To adapt to change means to learn new information and be able to comfortably use it. To learn all the information in the occupations shown above and below requires somebody who can teach that information. Despite all the controversy about the amount and quality of American education, the fact is we need to learn a lot about ourselves and how to adapt to change. The information these changes carry will ensure long term job stability for good teachers. They will need a much higher degree of training in literacy, science and mathematics than is presently the case.

Traditionally, teaching enjoys growth during depressions. As property values fall and property taxes are defaulted, there will be some cutbacks in the pay and numbers of public school teachers, but generally, the demand for education enjoys growth during U.S. depressions. This trend will last for ten years before it slows.

Computer programmers and analysts

This field is expected to grow from the late 1980's right through 1995, depression or no depression. The Bureau of Labor Statistics expect computer fields including programmers, operators, service technicians and systems analysts to grow every year. As one example, there is plenty of work available for artificial intelligence programmers and people who can write in languages like ORACLE — a relational database management system. Ten years ago, ORACLE did not exist. The need for people to continue utilizing all the interactive abilities of computers will grow.

OPPORTUNITIES FOR NEW BUSINESS

We rely on new businesses to keep us working. Nearly 90% of all new jobs are created by businesses employing fewer than ten people. Many people respond to losing their jobs by starting their own small business. Past recessions in the United States led to higher numbers of new companies as the newly unemployed tried to make it on their own.

Since most American jobs are created by new businesses, it is important to project which businesses will successfully start up during the depression. The following areas will likely grow during the depression:

Repair and service technicians

As we run out of money to buy new consumer items, older models will increasingly require repair. Shoe repairers were in demand during the depression. With the move to recycling and repairing items we previously discarded, will come growth in tailoring, high quality second hand clothes, salvage, plumbing, carpentry and other repair work. This will be a growing area of self employment.

Equipment rental

As repair needs grow, many people will be unable to hire others to do necessary repairs. These people will borrow or rent tools, equipment, and vehicles. The fall in home construction and automobile sales combined with fewer jobs and less money will make us utilize our homes and automobiles more effectively than previously. Even so, many people will lose one or the other, or both. Housing and transportation will be rented out for shorter periods of time as people look for more ways of stretching limited resources.

Retail outlets

Thrift stores and pawn shops will flourish — along with stores selling seeds, home and gardening tools, sewing machines, food preservation and processing equipment, physical fitness, self-help, do-it-yourself and hobbies. Consignment stores will also grow. Many of these businesses will be run from people's homes using computers, telecommunications and shipping to tie everything together.

Computer based services

The depression will force many newly unemployed people to find other means of making an income. Many of them will become self-employed, offering the services they previously did at work. In some cases it is more efficient to work at home and send work in over the phone. Programmers and business professionals, especially those who can contribute to business functions or technical fields, will increasingly work at home.

Entertainment

Low cost family entertainment will surge during the depression as people look for ways to escape and occupy time. Inexpensively produced visual images from network, satellite, and cable television, video rentals, computer games and movies — especially drive-in movies, will grow in popularity. Night club attendance will go up — along with less expensive sporting and cultural events, gambling, alcohol and drug use.

With time and concern about how valuable we are to others, Americans will increase their emphasis on appearance and health. We will buy more low priced physical fitness and sports equipment. Inexpensive gymnasiums, dance studios and libraries will see increased patronage. Hobbies and home and garden improvement plans will abound.

Security

Crime blossoms with poverty and idle time. White collar fraud will proliferate. Domestic violence and criminal offenses will increase with growing economic and social tension. As more people lose their jobs and social service delivery systems are overwhelmed, a sense of desperation will set in, followed by a tragic surge in crime. Protecting ourselves from each other will lead to a boom in the sale of burglar alarms, locks, vaults, trained animals, weapons and other security systems.

Local manufacturing

The shrinkage of large American firms will be accompanied by the opening of small regional or local manufacturing firms. Using computer driven work sites and other equipment that improves flexibility, these firms will make many different items for a variety of industries. These firms will compete effectively with foreign companies rendered less efficient in smaller markets by the depression. They will be located in smaller towns and cities having lower costs and a higher quality of living than major cities.

Skilled crafts

High quality craft and machine work will be introduced to compete with foreign made goods. Crafts which become less expensive than foreign machine made products will be successful. Look for handmade clothing, furniture, and toys to come more into vogue. This will also reflect an renewed interest in quality and goods that last longer.

PERSONAL EMPLOYMENT PROSPECTS

Assess your present position

To find your employment prospects in the midst of changes in historical employment patterns and with regard to the oncoming depression, ask yourself the following questions:

1. How secure is my present job?
2. Do I like my work?
3. Am I good at what I do?

If you choose to change your life, then you can prepare with one of the following actions:

1. Change Jobs
2. Drop Out of Society
3. Get an Education
4. Change Careers
5. Retrain
6. Relocate for Work
7. Start a Business

4. If I had to apply for my job today, would I be hired?
   a. If so, why would my company hire me?
   b. If not, why not?
5. Can a machine or computer be built to do my work?

If the answer to the first question is, "Not very secure," or if the answer to questions 2-5 is "No," or if you are not sure about the answer to questions 4a or 4b, your employment prospects for the coming depression need improvement. Ask yourself:

6. What attributes do I bring to a company?
7. How do I excel?
8. How can I improve my chances?

PERSONAL CHOICES

Primary personal life choices appear below. Choose one:

❑ **A.** Do nothing and wait for the inevitable.

❑ **B.** Change your life.

If you choose B, then you have several more decisions to make on the facing page . . .

If you think you can be replaced within the next five years, (ten years if you are under age 45), your employer may feel the same way. The coming depression may make this a reality much sooner. Preparing now will improve your chances during the coming hard times.
Each person's needs differ, but certain common elements include:

*Personal desires
*Personal finances — The longer you can live with lessened or no income, the more options you have
*Family member desires
*Family responsibilities
*Ties to friends and communities

After assessing your current position, if you need a change, follow the four steps outlined in detail below:

1. Research your options
2. Outline your future
3. Develop a written plan
4. Implement your plan

To go to school or start a business requires time and money. It requires at least a year's income, financial or government aid, or some other means of paying expenses while attending classes. For most people, although education is a necessity, this type of financial backing is very difficult to find. However, the means to explore your options at no cost exists for most Americans, especially those living in large cities.

By utilizing these four steps, you can develop an accurate means of assessing, planning, and implementing education and career choices that will help your family and you be happier and more secure.

Step One: Research your options

Good research translates into increased knowledge and subsequent career satisfaction and happiness. Determine what you need to enhance your employability. Learn about job trends and the economy. Set a time limit to learn what you need to know, but preferably no more than four to six weeks as time is short. Ask your family and friends their opinions. Go to your local library and ask for the librarian's help with your research. Go to school administrators or your local municipality for help determining what skills you should learn, courses to take, competition, times and costs.

Pursue information from your contacts including friends, relatives, classmates, and employers until you are satisfied with your mental picture of what fields and jobs you wish to enter. Then take this information and turn it into a written plan.

Step Two: Outline your future

What is my/our career future presently and over the next ten years?

_____

_____

_____

Will my family or I be changing jobs or careers?

_____

_____

_____

_____

_____

_____

Will these changes involve:
  a. Moving?

_____

_____

  b. Education for myself or others in the family?

_____

_____

_____

  c. Changing jobs?

_____

_____

_____

How much will this cost?

_____

_____

How will the family's situation be changed by following the plan?

_____

_____

_____

_____

Who will be affected personally? (list all family members)

_____

_____

_____

_____

What is the financial impact?

_____

_____

_____

Will these changes strengthen or hurt the family?

_____

_____

_____

Are there alternatives?

_____

_____

_____

How does every family member feel about this? (Let every family member write in his or her own answers)

_____

_____

_____

_____

_____

_____

_____

_____

_____

_____

_____

Timing:
  a. How long does it take to implement this plan?

_____

_____

  b. When does it begin?

_____

_____

  c. Will the family suffer while this plan is underway?

_____

_____

_____

  d. How long before there is an improvement?

_____

_____

What else needs to be addressed? (Let your family members contribute topics. Ask your friends and people you respect for help with this.)

_____

_____

_____

Step Three: Develop a written plan

Allow family members and others whose opinion you respect to write in their remarks. Then write all this information into a plan and present it to everyone affected by it. Everyone over the age of five will have some level of understanding and concern with this type of planning. It will also bring up other areas that need to be addressed. Consequently, it will pay for you to develop short term goals regarding the type of skills you have and subsequent careers you can enter within eighteen months. Consider using these short term skills as stepping stones to your long term goals. For example, learn electronics technology as a springboard to becoming an electrical engineer. Look for technical fields that will give you hands-on experience while building up to higher goals.

Step Four: Implement your plan

Depressions often lead to self-improvement. Those who realize the importance of acting now and follow through with their plans will have an advantage over those who wait for the depression to hit with full force. To move quickly now will have its payoffs, but it may mean sacrifices in your current lifestyle in the hopes of improving your future.

When material values fall, it makes sense to invest in yourself. Skills and education that enhance your employability will make you more valuable to others and, quite often, to yourself. Life with meaningful work is far more fulfilling than life without work.

Retraining and advanced education

One way in which you can help "job proof" yourself is to develop the skills necessary to make you always employable. Pick a field you like and take responsibility for learning your way into this field. As you learn, take a look at how your education can be used to broaden your means of employability. In other words, diversify your knowledge. Learning to type makes it far easier to use a computer. Computer skills apply to virtually every area. American business will require two broad areas of skill from its employees: 1) A high level of technical training, and 2) The motivation to continually retrain and learn new skills.

The depression will eliminate jobs for working class wage earners and improve the careers of technical and some professional workers. To change careers or attend school is a hard and often risky choice to make. When other peoples' lives are involved, as they usually are, the contemplated changes are often frightening.

Few people will make the sacrifices necessary to change their lives for an unseen future. Consequently, those who do, will have more choices available to them.

EDUCATION — THE BEST CHOICE

In order to compete in a tight market you must utilize the available resources to their best advantage. For the United States — and the world — the coming basis of competition will be the productive use of brain power. With or without the depression, the trend is to more educated workers, making higher level decisions, carrying far more responsibility and operating much more independently.

Japan, with one quarter the population of the U.S., employs five times as many engineers as the United States. Three quarters of the science and engineering majors, two-thirds of the graduate students and one-half of the Ph.D's in the American universities come from foreign countries.

The present generation of Americans is less literate than the last. Sixty million Americans are functionally illiterate. Almost half of all American students do not complete high school. Yet technology and global competition call for higher skills than ever before. To handle the information age, to run the latest manufacturing technologies, and to start businesses able to compete in the world market calls for high level skills. The law of supply and demand states that what is rare is valuable. Today, education is rare. To survive requires investing in yourself and the lives of those around you.

Most of the good jobs in the future will require post secondary school education. The growing fields mentioned earlier in this chapter will give you some idea of the types of skills needed by business during the depression. It is important to understand that management and staff will need a broad array of talents. Concentrate on one area, but keep your mind open. A programmer unable to communicate is less employable than one who can. For those whose life circumstances afford them the privilege of getting a good education, now is an excellent time to get one. It will stand you in good stead with regard to income and self esteem over time.

CHANGE JOBS, START A BUSINESS?

The purpose of business is to find and keep customers. If your plans involve working for another company or starting your own business, customers represent the bottom line. As the country continues to move towards a service based economy, service to the customer — whether it comes as quality on the production line or how employees interact with the public — will be of paramount importance. Look for quality in your work and the company for whom you intend to work.

Major considerations include: How likely it is for another employer — or yourself if you decide to go into business on your own — to stay in business during the coming depression? Does the employer provide an essential product or service that will continue to be purchased during a time of scarce money? Is the business elastic? Will it survive a shock? Would it contract by laying people off, lowering pay, shortening hours or all three? Does the business appear concerned about the welfare of its employees? Is it well run?

The more questions you answer, the easier it will be to make hard choices. Remember, a good information base will make you feel more secure when it is time to take action.

The technological changes already underway around the world and the coming depression will strongly alter how we work and where we live. Most of us will change careers several times during our lifetimes. The depression will bring home the importance of education and the shakiness of less skilled work.

To drop everything, change jobs or careers, and possibly relocate is not only difficult, but it can play havoc with home life. A new job or business requires family flexibility and hard work. However, those who do plan and try to question their present activities will be actively working, rather than giving in to despair and fear.

Chapter
8
Lifestyle Changes

Preparing for the depression requires making positive changes in the way you live. This chapter outlines some of the changes you can make that will promote your all around development. By adapting your lifestyle and attitudes now, you will be better able to live through hard times without experiencing overwhelming distress. Even a depression does not have to be depressing. The changes that will prepare you include:

1. Simplifying your life
2. Growing beyond materialism
3. Developing an independent sense of self-esteem
4. Improving your health through diet, exercise, and humor
5. Learning techniques of stress management

In making these changes, keep in mind that you need to concentrate on the aspects of your life you can control. At this point, you have little or no control over global economic changes. Perhaps you will have no control over whether or not you lose your job. However, you do have control over your personal habits, behavior, and mental attitude. Concentrating your efforts in these controllable aspects of life will make you much less vulnerable to frustration and despair, both of which make positive action more difficult.

If you wait until you are forced to change your lifestyle, you risk feeling bitter and dejected. Voluntarily making the necessary changes now is physically and mentally healthier. When you are in control, you sail your own ship. Waiting for trouble forces you to react from crisis to crisis, rather than acting independently and creatively to plan your own life.

SIMPLIFICATION

Do you feel that your life is too complex to get a handle on what is really going on? Do you have a nagging sense of innumerable "loose ends" that swirl around waiting to snag you? Do you ever feel that your possessions own you and not the other way around?

The complexity and pace of modern life grows daily. If you answered yes to any of these questions, you are in good company. According to a Louis Harris survey, 90% of Americans report experiencing high stress and 60% report feeling "great stress" at least once or twice a week.[1] Failure to make a conscious effort to order our lives in a simpler and more manageable way leaves us at the mercy of outside forces, much like swimming in a tidal wave.

Simplifying life takes a different form for each individual. For some it may mean giving up a vehicle they rarely use; for others it may mean paying off credit cards and having fewer bills to pay. Giving away clothes you seldom wear and selling appliances you don't really need are other ways to simplify your life. For Henry David Thoreau, it meant living a tranquil life by the side of Walden Pond. He wrote:

In short, I am convinced, both by faith and experience, that to maintain one's self on this earth is not a hardship but a pastime, if we will live simply and wisely.[2]

Is your home filled with clutter? If so, your mind may reflect a similar clutter. Many people are amazed when they move at how much stuff they own. Much of it they obviously don't need, or they would have been more aware of it. Pretend you are going to move and go through all your miscellaneous possessions, giving away or selling everything that holds no real significance to you. Many of us have dozens of books and records that we know we will never read or listen to again. Give them to the used book sale at the local library, donate them to a poor overseas school, or trade them in for other used books and records that you really want and will use. The fewer things you have, the freer you will feel.

Consider limiting the new stuff you bring into your life. Don't buy things just because they are on sale. Every unneeded object you buy, no matter how impressive the discount, is no bargain. Madison Avenue may say something is new and improved; that doesn't mean your old one will not meet your needs just as well. Corporate product developers and marketers will always come up with something else and flood airwaves and billboards with clever manipulation to convince you your life will be better with Brand X and Product Z. But the true quality of your life — what really matters — does not change.

Food, transportation, and services all offer a wealth of possibilities for simplifying your life. Cooking simpler, less processed, more nutritious meals is healthier and cheaper. Sharing a car with a friend or taking public transportation will cause some inconvenience, but the mental stress and money you save will pay many cab fares and allow you to rent a car when you really need one and still have a lot of money left over. How many of the services you pay for, could you do yourself or learn? When hard times arrive, you may be forced to do without outside paid service providers. Learn to do it now and avoid the rush; check out do-it-yourself books from the library. Learning easy auto maintenance, basic carpentry, sewing and yard work can all be personally satisfying as well as help to increase your savings.

Keep in mind what is really important to you as you design your own plan for simplification. Do not sacrifice what you are not ready to give up. When you let go, do it freely. Austerity is a joy for some, and for others an unbearable deprivation. Don't let someone else's standards dictate your own choices. What is a luxury for one person may be a necessity for another. A doctor may need a reliable late model car to be sure he'll be able to respond in an emergency, whereas for someone else it may be just a status symbol. The more you develop your own sense of the liberating effect of simplification, the happier you will be, regardless of economic crisis.

To assist in the process of simplification, complete the following chart.

Type of Possession	Necessary	Unnecessary	Method of Disposal	Date of Disposal
_____	_____	_____	_____	_____
_____	_____	_____	_____	_____
_____	_____	_____	_____	_____
_____	_____	_____	_____	_____
_____	_____	_____	_____	_____
_____	_____	_____	_____	_____
_____	_____	_____	_____	_____
_____	_____	_____	_____	_____
_____	_____	_____	_____	_____
_____	_____	_____	_____	_____
_____	_____	_____	_____	_____
_____	_____	_____	_____	_____
_____	_____	_____	_____	_____

First list the type of possession, then whether it is necessary or unnecessary, how you will dispose of it (i.e. donate to a thrift store, sell, toss, etc.), and the date you will do it by.

GROWING BEYOND MATERIALISM

True security comes from knowing who you really are and developing genuine relationships with people that are based upon your inner knowledge. The sense of self worth and safety that comes from the unconditional love of family, friends, and your true self can never be destroyed or taken from you. Even if the people you love die or move away, a sense of harmony remains once you have firmly established it. In hard times, this inner peace will insure your emotional survival and prevent you from being a depressed casualty.

The attempt to measure happiness by our bank account or possessions will always fail. The more we value things over human relationships, spiritual and emotional health, the more we delude ourselves and the less happy we become. No possession is immune from the dangers of theft, damage, fire, and time. Every day we observe the transitory nature of all things, both animate and inanimate. Change is the constant for all creation. Relying with certainty on the ever changing can only bring disappointment in the long run. The shiny sports car we think we love could be totalled tomorrow and will some day be another blotchy rusted shell in an auto graveyard on the edge of town.

Our society fosters the cult of acquisition through advertising and popular entertainment. A shocking truth few people are aware of is the pervasiveness of subliminal advertising with its manipulation of our psyches through sex and violence. Advertisements for products such as alcohol and cigarettes contain hidden images of skulls, knives, and sexuality. It is no accident that we learn to equate happiness with things.

The beer those attractive young men and women are drinking is supposed to make you feel better too. For only $15,000, you can drive the car that brings the opposite sex swarming. Your dream house in suburbia is supposed to ensure that your family will live happily ever after. But that beer won't make you younger, the car won't make you sexier, and the home in suburbia will fulfill no worthwhile dreams if it isn't filled with love.

The average teenager will have watched 350,000 television commercials by the time he or she graduates from high school. Every week our minds and our children's minds are assaulted by 1,500 advertisements. Ads for stimulants, headache cures, cold remedies, tranquilizers, and sleeping pills send the message that all of life's problems can be solved by taking a pill. Is it any wonder that the proliferation of drugs continues to be one of our society's biggest concerns? Most of us think, "Aw, those commercials don't affect me. I never pay any attention to them." Consciously, we may not notice commercials, but our subconscious and the even more vulnerable minds of our kids soak it all in.

Mass media fosters the mistaken belief that material wealth is the same as happiness. The day Ed McMahon calls your name and the ten million dollars is yours will not bring real happiness. Lottery and sweepstakes winners solve only temporary material problems; their existing emotional and family difficulties are not solved. In his book, *Wealth Addiction*, Philip Slater describes the unhappy state of many of the world's wealthiest people. Their wealth is often an addiction that gives them less pleasure as they strive to accumulate more.

[In a shipwreck] one of the passengers fastened a
belt about him with two hundred pounds of gold in it, with which he was
afterwards found at the bottom. Now, as he was sinking — had he the
gold? Or had the gold him?
> — Ruskin

Money is a tool, something you use to accomplish a task. Our society fosters the belief that the attainment of wealth is a worthy goal in itself, irrespective of any notable task for which it may be used. This glorification of accumulation for its own sake has created a climate of greed and selfishness. When those whose greed is the most out of control become celebrated and revered, it is clear that the disease of "wealth addiction" is contagious.

For the last 22 years, college freshmen have been surveyed regarding their basic attitudes. The most recent results show that 75% of 290,000 entering freshmen list "being well off financially" as a top goal, the highest in the history of the survey.[3] Rather than seeing greed as a destructive sickness, it is perceived as an acceptable means to a laudable goal — making as much money as possible as fast as possible.

Growing beyond materialism and reversing this trend is not an easy task. Conscious decisions must be made to examine yourself and your priorities. What makes you happy? Is happiness a temporary state of sense gratification, or is it a more permanent state of being and understanding? Does money and the things it can buy lead you any closer to real happiness? What changes do you need to make to lessen the role that acquisition plays in your life?

Fame or one's own self, which matters to one most?
One's own self or things bought, which should count most? In the
getting or the losing, which is worse?
Hence he who grudges expense pays dearest in the end;
He who has hoarded most will suffer the heaviest loss.

Be content with what you have and are, and no one can
    despoil you;
Who stops in time nothing can harm.
He is forever safe and secure.
                    — Lao Tzu from the *Tao Te Ching*[4]

To achieve the balance of Lao Tzu, we need to put the material things in our lives into proper perspective. The enjoyment of our possessions comes from within us, not from the thing itself. Being content with who we are and what we possess is an inner quality that is truly priceless. You can work to achieve that contentment by making a conscious effort to share with others. What feels better — keeping something to yourself or experiencing the delight and gratitude of the person you share it with? Practice giving something or doing something for someone with no thought of return. This sort of selfless service has the power to open your heart and allow you to receive an intangible reward that brightens your life more than an expected return. Experiment with letting go of expensive things by seeing how you feel with and without them.

The things that we live with every day become extensions of ourselves, and the loss of them can create stress, grief, and a feeling of sadness. These are real feelings that you must acknowledge in order to put losses behind you and move ahead. To a lesser extent, but similar to the loss of someone we care about, the process of dealing with the loss of things that are important to us involves fully experiencing our feelings, then releasing them, and finally moving ahead through positive action. Talking with a trusted friend or counselor about our feelings can also be an essential part of the letting go and the healing.

Learning how to let go of the things we hold dear is a vital aspect of growing beyond materialism. When we come closer to the contentment and balance of Lao Tzu, we will be well prepared for the loss of possessions the depression will bring to many. The key is to learn more about ourselves and consciously nurture what it is within that makes us happy.

SELF-ESTEEM

It has become accepted to equate our self esteem with our appearance or our career. In the words of sociologist David Riesman, we have become "other-directed," giving more importance to the opinions and perceptions of others than we give to our own. Comedian Billy Crystal's character Fernando sums up this obsession in his hilarious line, "Remember, it is more important to look good than to feel good." This national mania has created multibillion dollar industries in cosmetics, plastic surgery, fitness fads, tanning salons, and fingernail shops.

Defining ourselves by our job is also common. Next to the perfunctory, "How are you?" the question most often asked when meeting a stranger is, "What do you do?" Nothing seems to matter more than the job that you spend eight hours a day doing. Defining yourself and others by a paying job sets you up for a potentially catastrophic loss of self-esteem. If your job or business is lost and you have difficulty finding a new one, you may feel diminished as a human being. Numerous studies of the chronically unemployed show a plummeting sense of self-worth that can lead to severe abuse of oneself and others.

Basing self-esteem on your inner self and unique qualities is healthier than focusing on your appearance or your job. Every human being has many qualities that make him or her special. For example, a sincere sparkling smile, a good sense of humor, an ability to listen well, an empathy for fellow human beings, children, plants or animals, an inquisitive mind, creative talent, a capacity for devotion, and the energy for helping others represent positive qualities that come from within. Take a good look at your special gifts and work to develop and nurture them.

Start the process by developing a list of what you value about yourself:

_____

_____

_____

Then write down ways you can nurture these qualities:

_____

_____

_____

Examples of ways to nurture your valuable qualities might be that you will take a class to challenge and develop your mental abilities or that you will nurture your love for people by volunteering at a local food bank.

The best way to foster self-esteem is by getting in touch with your deepest self and harmonizing your actions with your guiding principles. This inner development is discussed extensively in the next chapter.

HEALTH

Improving your health is an essential part of preparing for hard times; good diet and fitness habits will bring immediate benefits as well as prepare you for future challenges. According to a study by the Centers for Disease Control, over 52% of premature deaths were caused by unhealthy lifestyle.[6] When the tangible items of your life are jeopardized, maintaining a healthy lifestyle and body will be even more important to you. The aspects of health described in this section are diet, fitness, and humor.

Eat smarter

Eating smarter involves developing healthy attitudes towards food and consciously planning what to eat and what to avoid. To eat smarter you need to learn about basic nutrition, develop a sense of how food affects you, create a plan for eating better, and — most importantly — follow through on your plan. Don't forget that eating is an opportunity for pleasure. Eating smarter can be a lot of fun as you experiment with new kinds of food and ways of eating. Don't be scared into not making positive changes in your diet because you think it will take some pleasure out of your life. Dieting may not be fun, but eating a better diet can be.

Learn about basic nutrition

Getting the information you need about nutrition is easy. Any library, book store, or health food store has a wide variety of books on nutrition. Although every book presents a unique perspective, you'll find that the basic facts about what nutrients you need to attain and maintain a healthy diet are consistent. When you purchase a car or a new appliance, you read the owner's manual to see how it operates and what maintenance is required. Consider your research on nutrition to be like reading the owner's manual for your own body. Other ways to learn more about what your body needs include taking a class, consulting with a nutritionist, and viewing films or videos on nutrition.

Food is the fuel our bodies and minds need to function properly. Eating nutritious food in moderate amounts gives the energy you need to live and prevents the development of food related illness. Conversely, eating certain foods in excess takes energy from our body and leads to disease. More and more illnesses have been found to be directly linked to the food we eat. Among the major health problems that have a dietary link are heart disease, cancer, diabetes, and hypertension. Cancer researchers estimate that lifestyle factors including diet contribute to about 35% of all cancer deaths. Two of the most hazardous substances found in food are fat and cholesterol. The largest quantities of both are found in meat, eggs, and dairy products. They should be eaten only in moderation, and there is growing evidence that a vegetarian diet is one of the healthiest.

Develop a sense of how food affects you

Each person is different and reacts to food in a unique way. What is healthy food for one person may cause a severe reaction in another. You need to learn more about how different foods and ways of eating affect you. You can do this in a variety of ways. Listen to what your body tells you. Constipation, diarrhea, gas, insomnia, bad dreams, headaches, colds, indigestion, heartburn, sluggishness, and nervousness can all be signs that something in your diet may be out of balance with what you need. Experiment with eliminating certain foods to see if your health improves. In addition to what you eat, other possible contributing factors include how much you eat, when you eat, and what combinations of food you eat.

Sorting out all of the possible factors can be complicated and may require the help of a professional, perhaps a doctor or nutritionist. However, many doctors receive only minimal training in nutrition and may be reluctant or unable to establish a dietary link to a health problem. If you have reason to believe your problem may be related to diet, seek out a doctor who is experienced in nutrition. Many osteopaths, chiropractors, homeopaths, and other "natural healers" have received extensive training in dietary links to disease. Through the use of kinesiology (a form of muscle testing) and allergy testing, you may discover foods that are detrimental to your physical and mental health.

Create a plan for eating better

When you have learned more about nutrition and how different foods affect you, you are ready to develop your own personal plan for eating smarter. Take into account both your body's needs for health and vitality and what is detrimental to your health. The elements of your plan may include the following:

✔ *Which foods and combinations of food you need*
✔ *Which foods and combinations of food you should avoid*
✔ *When you should eat*
✔ *How much you should eat*
✔ *How often you should eat*
✔ *Which foods you like to eat*
✔ *Which foods you don't like to eat*

Some people like to plan specific weekly menus for all meals. Others prefer to spontaneously decide what to eat at a particular time or to see what's in the refrigerator. One advantage of advance planning is you can shop more efficiently and save some money.

Rather than attempting to change your whole diet overnight, gradually adjust and wean yourself from less healthy foods. Generally, moderate changes in lifestyles will take hold better and be more permanent than crash diets or overly restrictive regimens. Remember to treat your changes in your eating habits as an adventure and have fun.

Follow through on your plan

Sticking to your plan is the key to eating smarter. The popularity of hundreds of diet books and plans attests to the fact that people often have a difficult time following through on diets. Otherwise they wouldn't be constantly trying another new diet that may be magically easier to follow than the last one was. One reason for overeating is stress. A study in the *Ladies Home Journal* reports that 74% of women overeat because of stress.[7] Read the section on stress management later in this chapter for ideas on how to cope with this problem.

Another reason for the difficulty in following a diet plan is that, for many, food is an addiction as potent as any drug. Among the most effective ways to break an addiction is through a support group. Weightwatchers and Overeaters Anonymous are two well known organizations that function as effective support groups for many people. Just as Alcoholics Anonymous has helped millions deal with their dependency on alcohol, groups such as these help decrease a dependency on eating too much or eating the wrong foods. Perhaps the most important support group for helping you follow through on your personal plan is your own family. The love, acceptance, and reinforcement they can give to help you maintain your plan is enormous. Even better is if the family develops the plan together and supports each other in following through.

Another effective way to combat a negative addiction is to replace it with a positive habit. Developing a routine that becomes an essential part of your life can replace the craving for food with one that contributes to your health. We all know people who regularly jog, do aerobics, play racquetball, or ride a bicycle. As long as it is not carried to an extreme that endangers health, this is a positive habit that brings benefit. Other positive habits can include writing, painting, meditating, sewing, crafts, music, and hobbies. If you develop consuming interests in activities that enrich your life, it is much easier to break a consuming interest in food.

Diet and hard times

Unfortunately, rather than paying more attention to their diets in hard times, many people neglect them. Reports from the last Depression describe many families who used their extremely limited resources for nutritionally poor food. Candy makers often report increased sales in times of economic decline as people forced to forego the bigger luxuries indulge in smaller ones, like a hot fudge sundae or piece of apple pie ala mode. When people are depressed, they eat more junk food. Be especially diligent in following your eating smarter plan when other areas of your life are difficult. Following through on your plan will give you a healthy consistency in something over which you have control.

Fitness

A program of regular exercise greatly improves your overall health and resistance to disease. Improving your physical fitness is a vital part of getting ready for the challenges of hard times. A fit person is more physically and mentally able to thrive in a time of scarcity and rapid change. Fitness does not require hours a day. Professional athletes and models may need to pump iron and workout constantly, but most of us will feel and look better with a moderate amount of effort.

For cardiovascular well being, strenuous aerobic exercise for at least 20 minutes three to five times a week is recommended.[8] The best type of aerobic exercise for cardiovascular development involves continuous motion. Among the best are cross country skiing, swimming, jogging, dance, brisk walking and aerobic workouts. Activities that involve a lot of stopping and starting like football, softball, and tennis will improve muscle tone but benefit your cardiovascular system much less. The major benefits of regular exercise include the following:

* Increases endurance
* Helps lose weight through burning of calories and a natural
            suppression of appetite
* Lowers blood pressure
* Delays loss of calcium in bones, can help prevent osteoporosis
* Helps dissipate symptoms of stress
* Conditions your heart to operate more efficiently

Another type of exercise that can be beneficial is the regular practice of yoga. Yoga postures are part of the ancient science of yoga which is designed to harmonize physical, mental, and spiritual development. The beneficial effects of yoga include a regulation of the glandular system, deep relaxation, improved flexibility and muscle tone, and a heightened sense of inner peace. You can learn yoga from a book, but it is more beneficial to learn from an experienced instructor. Many recreational centers include yoga courses in their offerings. In most metropolitan areas, you can find an instructor by looking up Yoga in the yellow pages.

Develop a regular fitness program

If you do not already have a regular fitness routine, consider starting one. Exercise as simple as continuous walking can give you as much cardiovascular aerobic work as you need. Bicycling is an example of exercise that is relatively easy to start, can save you money for transportation, and is a lot of fun. The recreational and social aspect of exercise also deserves attention. If you see your fitness as fun, you are much more likely to reorder your life to include it on a regular basis.

Six steps to design your fitness program:

1. Assess the current state of your fitness. You can do this by having a comprehensive physical exam from your doctor or a free fitness analysis at a local health club that is eager for your membership.

2. Determine some measurable fitness goals. For instance, if you can run for ten minutes comfortably, set a goal of increasing to 20 minutes in a month's time.

3. Decide which activities you prefer. As long as you are getting enough of an aerobic workout and the risk is minimal, it really does not matter what type of exercise you choose.

4. If you are older than forty or have any significant health problems, you should consult your physician before you get much further. Tell him or her what you have in mind and get an opinion as to its suitability for your situation.

5. Make a schedule for your regular exercise. Put it on your calendar or some other prominent place, like your refrigerator.

6. Get started. Remember that warmups are necessary to minimize the risk of injury. Periodically review your plan and adjust it as necessary. Last but not least, enjoy it.

Humor

By now you are thinking about eating healthier food and pulling out your old sweat suit. If the prospect of giving up your sedentary ways and cheeseburgers is sobering, you are ready for the third component of your health program — humor, also known as laughter, yucks, knee slappers, chuckles, wit, and just plain goofing around.

The connection between humor and health has always been known, but only recently has it been studied. The Bible says, "A cheerful heart does good like medicine: but a broken spirit makes one sick."[9] Lightheartedness helps to distance your self from your troubles. Norman Cousins, who cured himself of a crippling spinal injury through liberal doses of jokes and Marx Brothers movies, thinks that laughter may stimulate the production of endorphins, the body's own natural painkiller. He said, "What was significant about the laughter. . . [was] that it creates a mood in which the other positive emotions can be put to work, too. In short, it helps make it possible for good things to happen."[10]

Look for positive opportunities to laugh everywhere. Make a practice of seeking a joke or humorous incident every day. Places to look for humor include the newspaper comics, joke books, funny calendars, comedy clubs, cartoons, Dial-A-Joke, movies, talking with your children, and *The Congressional Record.*

Some of the funniest material is all around you and is not labeled as humor . . . your daily life. All of the twists, surprises, and indignities of life can be cause for humor if seen in the right light. One of the world's most absurd comedians, Mullah Nasrudin, the Sufi mystic, was renowned as a saintly fool. One day he was searching for something beneath a street light. His feverish efforts drew a crowd. Someone asked him what he was doing, and he replied he was looking for his keys. "Where did you lose them?" one bold youth shouted. "Why somewhere over there," he answered pointing off in the distance. The incredulous crowd was bewildered. Finally, a man spoke up, "Why then, are you looking for them here?" To which the Mullah calmly answered, "There's more light here."

Healthy people focus on kind humor as opposed to sarcastic, negative, ethnic, put down, and cruel humor. There is plenty to smile and laugh about in the human condition that is not created at the expense of someone else. That kind of humor will not raise your spirit.

The mental and physical rewards of laughing at yourself and the world will nicely complement your changing diet and fitness. In the last depression, laughter was a lifeline for millions, and it will serve the same purpose in the hard days to come.

When the heart weeps for what it has lost, the spirit laughs for what it has found. — anonymous Sufi aphorism

STRESS MANAGEMENT

Stress is the scourge of the industrial age. It is a concept that was virtually unheard of before rapid industrialization and the added pressures brought on by living and working with machines at a speeded up pace of life. Although the concept is new to the 20th century, stress has always been a part of life.

The most widely accepted definition of stress was put forth by Hans Selye, the pioneering stress researcher. He defined stress as "the nonspecific response of the body to any demand upon it." Selye tracked this nonspecific response through physiological reactions in the glandular, nervous, and circulatory systems. Selye described how stress works in the human body through the General Adaption Syndrome or GAS, which produces a fight or flight response. Without effective coping, this response leads to a stage of resistance and then exhaustion, which creates a state where the body is vulnerable to a wide variety of illnesses.[11]

A stressor is an outside influence that creates stress in an individual. Among the most common stressors in modern life are the pressures of work, family problems, financial worries, and traffic jams. Every individual reacts to these stressors differently, and it is important to realize that stress is not all bad. Stressors that lead to an ulcer or mental breakdown for one person may create the level of stress that someone else needs to be stimulated and challenged. Prolonged unemployment is a very difficult stressor to cope with; the depression will increase this and others.

Among the most common diseases and disorders that result from stress are heart disease (affecting 30 million Americans), high blood pressure (affecting 25 million Americans), ulcers (affecting 8 million Americans), and drug and alcohol abuse. An estimated 12 million Americans are alcoholics.[12] Fifteen percent of the population suffer from serious mental disorders.[13]

Coping is the key to stress. Through physical methods such as regular exercise, yoga, diet, and breathing exercises, many people are better able to handle stress. Mental techniques for dealing with stress include meditation, prayer, biofeedback, getting in touch with feelings, genuine communication, listening to soothing music, and counseling. Others deal with stress by attempting to remove the stressor or avoiding situations that are stressful to them.

Steps to stress management

Initiating your own program of stress management now will pay great dividends during the society-wide stress of hard times. Investigate the various methods for dealing with stress and experiment to find what works best for you. The following steps will help you in this process.

1. Evaluate your current level of stress and how it manifests. Do you have trouble sleeping, get frequent headaches, experience stomach aches unrelated to the food you eat, twitch nervously, or feel anxious on a regular basis? These are all signs of having difficulty dealing with stress.

2. Research the different techniques for stress management. There are hundreds of books available on the subject and many seminars. If you work for a large company, it may have stress management seminars available at no charge to you. Many corporations have Employee Assistance Programs with confidential counseling available to help you cope with work and life stress.

3. Decide which techniques feel the best for you. If you are unsure where to start, experiment with several to see which is right.

4. Once you have settled on a technique, set aside a regular time to practice. The habituation of your chosen technique will make it a much stronger source of comfort and strength.

Voluntarily adjusting your lifestyle will bring many immediate benefits and prepare you for a time when many will involuntarily adjust their lifestyles with bitter resignation. Making some of the recommended changes now may be the start of a glorious adventure that will lead you to a much different and happier way of living. When you learn to simplify, grow beyond materialism, enhance your self-esteem, improve your health, and better manage stress, you will be well prepared for the depression and the other challenges of living.

Endnotes

1. Louis Harris, *Inside America,* (New York: Vintage Press, 1987), p. 8.
2. Henry David Thoreau, *Walden,* (New York: New American, 1942), p. 53.
3. Mary Anne Dolan, *Universal Press Syndicate,* February 2, 1988.
4. Arthur Waley, *The Way and its Power,* (London: George Allen and Unwin, 1934), p. 197.
5. Mauden Nelson, *Essence,* June, 1986, p. 66.
6. Andrew J.J. Brennan, *Management World,* February, 1985, p. 13.
7. Barbara Sternberg, *Ladies Home Journal,* June, 1986, p. 6.
8. Harris, p. 13.
9. Nehemiah 8:10, RSV.
10. Norman Cousins, *Anatomy of an Illness,* (New York: Bantam Books, 1979), p. 48.
11. Martin Shaffer, *Life After Stress,* (New York: Plenum, 1982), pp. 14-16.
12. Edward N. Charlesworth and Ronald G. Nathan, *Stress Management,* (New York: Athenum, 1984), p. 10.
13. Robert Brown, *Department of Labor: U.S. House Committee on Appropriations,* 1986, p. 756.

Chapter
9
Inner Preparation

A vital but often neglected link in your chain of preparation is inner preparation. Attempting to order your finances, health, attitude, family, and community requires planning, effort, and reordering your priorities. But at least most of us have a frame of reference to begin the process and a concept of where we are heading. But inner preparation leads us to uncharted waters that don't appear on the maps that guide us from cradle to grave. The institutions we grow up with — including family, school, business, government, and sadly, religion — seldom give us the guidance we need to make the journey.

Each person has his or her own basic beliefs and guiding principles. The more expansive and positive these beliefs are and the better we are able to act in harmony with them, the more happiness we will experience. No matter how lofty and inspirational our beliefs are, if we fail to reflect them in our daily living, we will feel the pain that comes from separating ourselves from what we really want to be. The process of bringing our thoughts, words, and deeds into concert with our guiding principles is the most challenging and rewarding part of preparing for the depression. If we accomplish this, we will possess a peace and security that will not be disturbed by the dramatic changes swirling around us. This chapter will help you examine your guiding principles and develop a plan of action for the inner journey towards integrating them with your life.

DISCOVERING YOUR GUIDING PRINCIPLES

Your guiding principles may be based upon a particular religion or spiritual path you belong to or upon your own experience and study or a combination of the two. A person's guiding principles are often called spiritual beliefs or personal philosophy. You may think that the answers to the following questions are obvious because of your religious belief, but you will find it helpful to write down the answers and look at them. Unless you copy the answers right out of a book or scripture, your responses are bound to be different from anyone else's. The way each of us articulates and describes our own basic beliefs is part of what makes us unique.

Ask yourself the following questions and write your response in the space provided:

(Use additional paper if necessary, #2 pencils are not required)

Who Am I?

Why am I here?

What is the purpose of life?

Do I believe in God? (If your answer is no, feel free to skip the next questions)

Who or what is God?

How do I come closer to God?

Do I think God has a plan? If so, what do I think it is?

What do I think God wants me to do in this life?

What is death?

What do I think happens to me after I die?

Why is there pain and suffering?

What is real happiness? And how can I obtain it?

What is my responsibility towards other people?

What is my philosophy of life?

Additional statements of your beliefs:

Admittedly these are very difficult questions. Don't worry if you don't have a definitive answer for many of these questions. The idea is to find out where you are now. Many of your basic beliefs will change and evolve as you do. What made sense to you yesterday may not make sense today. Periodic confusion is a natural part of being alive. Through confusion we seek order, and finding order we are no longer confused. Also, if thinking about these questions brings up a lot of emotions, that too is natural. The eternal questions are not easy to contemplate, and that's why many people live their whole lives trying to avoid thinking about them.

Okay, let's assume you have gotten a handle on what your beliefs are. Now think about what there is in your guiding principles that will give you strength in a time of uncertainty. Does your faith in a higher power or in humanity or in yourself provide a foundation for seeing you through the depression in a positive way? Look specifically at which of your beliefs will help see you through the struggles to come.

Come up with your own list of strengthening beliefs:

1._____

_____

2._____

_____

3._____

4._____

_____

Now, what can you do to reinforce these beliefs and make them a daily reality that will give you strength to understand and deal with the depression?   For example:

* reading an appropriate scripture or inspirational book
* talking with a clergyperson
* discussing your beliefs with a family member, friend, fellow believer, or study group
* participating in a spiritual retreat
* going on a pilgrimage
* attending church or other spiritual functions more regularly
* praying or meditating
* helping those in need out of love
* setting a time aside each day to reflect on your guiding principles and reviewing how harmonious they are with your actions.

In your personal plan for inner preparation, try to focus on the more active methods of reinforcing beliefs. Actively working on yourself through a discipline like meditation or concentrated prayer will bring more positive change than sitting and listening to someone talk.

Write down actions you can take that correspond to your list of strengthening beliefs:

1._____

_____

_____

2._____

_____

_____

3._____

_____

4._____

_____

_____

These actions represent the elements of your plan for inner preparation. Now list them in priority order from the most important to the least important. For the top five actions write down how often you will perform them and for how long. You are making a commitment that essentially involves a contract between yourself and that inner guiding principle you hold dearest.

Here are some examples:

Name	Action	How Often	How Long	Date
Mark Friedman	Give 50% of my book profits to help the needy	Whenever I receive them	2 years	6/1/89
Mark Friedman	Meditate	Twice daily	Indefinitely	6/1
The Reader	_____	_____	_____	____
The Reader	_____	_____	_____	____
The Reader's Spouse	_____	_____	_____	____
The Reader's Child	_____	_____	_____	____

If you choose your commitments wisely and sincerely follow through on them, you will see positive changes in your life. Set a regular time to review your contract and change or renew your commitments. When an action becomes habitual, you can move on to other actions to work on with a conscious effort. Eventually you will accumulate an impressive array of invaluable inner tools designed by you to fit your needs. Share your contract with someone close to you and ask them to help remind you to follow through on your commitments. Perhaps they will be inspired by the idea and take up the practice also. There is the beginning of a support group.

Whether or not the depression comes in the manner you imagine, concentrating on deepening your beliefs and/or faith will bring ample rewards. If this process leads you to question your old beliefs and search for new ones, there are many avenues open for exploration. There are a wealth of individuals, books, and courses available that will help you explore options and choose your own path.

A word of caution however: Whenever possible, avoid spending large sums of money for so-called spiritual or esoteric instruction. With the burgeoning of the New Age movement, there are thousands of would-be psychics, channelers, seminar leaders, astrologers, palmists, lecturers, and healers who see an excellent opportunity to make many quick bucks off the anxiety and curiosity of sincere seekers. Some of these people may be legitimate, but true inner knowledge is not a commodity to be bought and sold. It is a fundamental birthright of human beings that should be as free as the air and sunlight.

Fellowship

An important aspect of inner preparation is the seeking of fellowship. The inner path is often steep and rocky. It is easy to stumble and fall time and time again. Having fellow travelers to accompany you on your journey is invaluable. They can help lift you up, dust you off, and help you on your way. The community of like minded travelers is tremendously nourishing and powerful. A spiritual community of sisters and brothers is the foundation for the renewal and expansion of faith. Especially if followers of your particular path are a minority in your community, fellowship will be the most important factor in your continued commitment. Without the liferaft of fellowship, you may find yourself cast adrift in a sea of conformity.

If you know no one in your community who is similarly interested in the inner journey, extend yourself to search others out. Here are a few ideas on how to go about this process:

✔ Read bulletin boards and classified ads for notices about seminars and meetings
✔ Place a small ad yourself inviting like minded individuals to a meeting.
✔ Discuss your beliefs with friends and acquaintances. You will be surprised at the number of people you know who are interested even though you would not have guessed.
✔ Take a class or teach a class through a local continuing education outlet.
✔ Browse through the appropriate section of your local bookstore, strike up conversations with people you meet there who share similar interests.
✔ Refer to the resource section at the back of the book.

After finishing the exercises in this chapter think carefully about how this inner preparation can be useful in your other depression planning. The inner strength you gain will make it easier to adjust your lifestyle and to reach out to your family and community. Happiness does not have to be slippery and elusive. The effort you expend to attain it will be replenished a hundred fold as you begin to feel the freedom that comes from harmonizing your actions and your guiding principles.

Chapter
10
The Importance of Family

The coming depression will expose the cracks in our society's foundation built upon material values rather than personal relationships. The beauty of beginning our depression preparation right in our own home is that everyone can start regardless of income. A shift in emphasis towards human values and relationships requires no money and will lead to increased savings and fulfillment in life.

The benefits of preparing your family for the depression will come regardless of the economic future. An emphasis on fostering basic family values such as working together, sharing, respect for all family members, helping others, direct and honest communication, and focusing on human and spiritual values instead of material values will yield emotional security that will last longer than either financial problems or prosperity.

THE CHANGING FAMILY

Families and the world as a whole have changed a great deal since the Depression of the 1930's. Some of these changes will help us cope with another depression, while others will put many of us at even greater risk, psychologically as well as financially.

The increase in divorce, the women's movement, and the trend to smaller households and greater personal freedom have created enormous changes in our social structure. Today, one in three households are headed by single women, and well over half of families headed by two spouses are two-income households. Our concept of "family" is rapidly changing to accommodate ex-spouses, step-children, and the bewildering array of relatives and relationships that accompany all of these changes.

We have begun to move toward a more equitable sharing of family and community tasks. Family income, for most, depends upon more than one person. Children benefit from attention and day-to-day care from fathers, relatives and other caregivers in addition to mothers. These changes will be of great benefit to us in the years ahead. As we will see, the interchange of roles and tasks is an essential ingredient to health and well-being in a depression economy.

Our standard of living is such that two incomes are often *required*. The number of single parents struggling to survive on low incomes has increased dramatically. They are often the hardest hit in difficult times because of the lack of social support and practical help. Other liabilities include the lack of adequate child care and children's afterschool programs, the substantial increases in costs of basic necessities such as medical care, and the breakdown of the extended family and neighborhood support systems.

In order to survive the depression and prosper with a measure of health and well-being, we will be required to change our attitudes about many things. Our ideas about money and its power in our lives will shift as will long-cherished concepts about the roles of various relationships, both in society and to us as individuals. Relationships take on new meaning during hard times.

In reality, your "family" may include many more people than your immediate relatives. Everyone in your support system is important to you, and thus in some ways interdependent. Your supportive network of friends, colleagues, and relatives is probably the most important "savings account" you own. How healthy is your support system today? Are there those who depend on you? How will your children handle the changes a depression might bring? Your parents? To what extent are you able to help and support people outside your immediate family?

WEAVING THE FAMILY SAFETY NET

In times of economic hardship, everyone needs a safety net. Despite high expenditures on federal social welfare and entitlement programs, the government will not be able to cover the cost of meeting our needs during the coming depression. The over two million presently homeless people in the United States, one-quarter of whom are children, aptly demonstrate this. The most rapid rise in homeless people is among families. During the depression their numbers will increase.

Families can become homeless when the breadwinner loses her or his work. Low paying jobs mean little or no savings and spending a disproportionate amount of income on housing. Families lacking relatives or friends to help them in their time of need end up on the streets or in shelters.

Now is the time for each of us to make sure that we do not find ourselves or our loved ones in such a predicament when the depression comes. The way to do this is to start now to strengthen our family ties and make contingency plans. The following steps will help in this process:

Assess the qualities of your family and extended family that will affect how all of you will survive the depression. Look for which family members will suffer the most and who will have the greatest ability to share with others. Who is in danger of losing their income or home?

Who can take others into their home? Do family members have special needs which the depression will make more difficult to meet?

Review the current state of your relationships with relatives and other "family" members. Take an objective and caring look at how you get along with your relatives. Examine both the quantity and quality of caring and communication with your parents, children, grandparents, aunts, uncles, cousins and other friends or people you care about. Are you concerned with their lives and they with yours? Are you happy with the level and extent of your relationship?

Reestablish contact with those with whom you have lost contact. Families usually have one member who diligently keeps track of all the far flung relatives. Ask her or him to send you the names, addresses and phone numbers of your relatives with whom you wish to reestablish contact. Track down old friends. Call them or send a letter and let them know you wish to reestablish contact. Share your hopes, dreams and concerns with them. Let them know you care. Try to reach all of your relatives and old friends. The idea is to weave a big net and enhance everyone's life at the same time.

Deepen the communication with your present relatives and friends. Sending birthday and holiday greetings with no deep communication is not enough to develop and maintain relationships that will prove mutually supportive during the rigors of the coming depression. Use the urgency of the situation to help you overcome your fear and let down your guard. Share your real feelings about them and yourself.

Offer information freely and tell them your concerns about the coming depression. If they lived through the last depression, draw them out and learn all you can about what it was like for them and how they coped.

Resolve old conflicts. Many families have painful incidents from the past that inhibit open, honest and loving relationships. Whenever possible, make the first move to deal with these issues by bringing them to the surface. This may prove difficult but can be exhilarating and strengthening. If the feelings are too deeply seated, ask another family member to help. The situation may require the assistance of outside or professional help to be resolved. If this is the case, you will have to determine if the effort is worthwhile.

Develop a written comprehensive plan based upon a realistic assessment of how you and other family members will be able to support one another during the depression. Plan on who will move into which house or who can loan you the money to make house payments if you lose your job. What if they lose their job also? Let those upon whom you are counting know your plans. Don't make assumptions based on a lack of information; the actual circumstances of your relatives and friends may be very different than you imagine.

Practice your plan. For example, if the plan is to take your sister and her family into your house, determine what space they will occupy and ask your children how they feel about this. Have the two families spend time together and, if possible, have them live briefly in your house to see how well it works and how to improve your plan.

The information you get from following the steps above will help you develop a realistic picture of how much help you can expect from your family and what help you can give them. It is important to learn this now and not wait until the depression begins. At that time, it may be much harder to ask for help. Further, the lack of preparation on the part of both yourself and your relatives may cause such requests to be met with more negative answers.

If your friends and relatives appear unlikely or unable to help you, you will have to look for resources in the neighborhood, churches or community. The next chapter will address how to develop these networks.

HOW DEPRESSIONS AND RECESSIONS AFFECT FAMILIES

Studies of the unemployed show that it is common for families to go through several stages after the main bread-winner loses a job. The first of these is denial (pretending everything is all right), which can be particularly acute in a family with a rigid lifestyle and fixed roles. With the end of this period of denial, usually around the twelfth month of unemployment, comes a critical period during which the incidence of substance abuse, child abuse, mental illness, separation and divorce increases considerably.

Stress is often the result of our expectations not being met. The "provider" expects the household to be taken care of, the homemaker expects the money to be there to pay the bills; the children expect to be provided with all the things their school or playmates have. One change — that of the provider losing his or her job — can ensure that all of these expectations are not going to be met. Without clear communication and the ability to re-group, the family can deteriorate very quickly.

Family survival traits

Dr. Robert C. Angell studied families through the Great Depression and discovered two key factors that lead either to family solidarity and adjustment or to disintegration during such a crisis. The first is *integration* — the degree to which family members support each other emotionally and economically, and to which they have common goals and interests. Naturally these factors differ for each family. Those with strong affectionate bonds fare the best. Common interests may include a shared spiritual or religious faith and commitment. Shared goals may include sending children to college or purchasing a family home. However, families which rely upon material goals and which do not regularly address the emotional needs of individual members are at risk.

Adaptability is another factor which can help or hinder a family's ability to weather a depression. A family's adaptability is basically an indicator of its underlying values. Those who depend greatly upon social status and material possessions or costly forms of recreation tend to become rigid and to cling to their standard of living as long as possible. Family members adhere to strict ideas about their roles and are unable to shift positions or reach out to each other and to helpers outside the family. This rigidity, on the part of any individual member or the whole group, can incapacitate the entire family in times of crisis. Family members may spend many months denying what is happening and trying to maintain their normal lifestyle, sinking further into debt in order to do so.

Integration and adaptability have a tremendous impact upon a family's vulnerability to the stress of a Depression economy. Dr. Angell's study showed that due to psychological factors alone, a 25% reduction in income for one family could be as devastating as a 75% reduction for another.

YOUR FAMILY'S EMOTIONAL PREPARATION FOR THE DEPRESSION

What can you do to increase your family's integration and adaptability? You have probably thought about what you would do in case of emergencies — fire, medical or natural disaster. Most families have insurance, perhaps smoke alarms and emergency phone numbers posted. But have you thought of economic disaster preparedness? The steps you can take now will cost little or nothing, and you have nothing to lose. Your psychological health as well as that of your family members is far more important, in the long run, than your bank account.

Step 1: Assess your family's emotional support system
To get an idea of how many people comprise your support system, make a list of all the people you, your spouse, and your children interact with on a regular basis that provide support. Include relatives, friends, neighbors, teachers, fellow church members, clergy, and co-workers. In a column next to their names, write down exactly what kind of support you get from them or give to them. For example, your neighbor may feed the dog and water your plants when the family goes on vacation. Your co-worker may always be willing to talk when something goes wrong at work. Your daughter and her friend may help each other with difficult homework assignments. Your clergy person may have provided spiritual counseling and support when a close friend died. You may have loaned your cousin $500 when his firm laid off 100 employees including him.

Name	Type of Support

Look closely at how much support your family has coming in and going out. An overall depth represents a degree of integration in your support structure that will be helpful to you in times of economic hardship. If you have an undeveloped support structure, think about ways you can interact with others that involve you with them emotionally and spiritually. The responsibility you have taken for those you love is important; expanding it to other areas of life not only enriches your relationships but builds security for you. Some of the hardest-hit people in the last Depression were men who felt their only value — to themselves, their relatives, friends, and colleagues — was as financial providers. Today we must begin to expand the concept of "provider" to include all of us. We provide material security for each other, and also more important provisions including warmth, attention, affection, and support for personal growth.

You also need a balance of incoming and outgoing emotional and spiritual energy. If you do most of the giving, a crisis can force you into depletion very rapidly, leaving you not only materially bankrupt but psychologically alienated as well.

Step 2: Expand your concept of family

Each of us needs to feel loved, connected to others, and needed by them. From the moment of birth, we begin to reach out to others and form attachments to fulfill our needs both to give and receive love. Our parents, brothers and sisters, relatives, friends, colleagues, spouses, children, even our pets are part of the fabric of love that supports our will to live and our sense of self-worth.

Each meaningful relationship fills a special place in our lives and is important to nurture and maintain. A healthy relationship involves give and take, strength and vulnerability, honesty and compassion. Having several relationships that grow in a balanced way is a goal that can be worked toward. Resolve today to bring people into your life that can nurture you and can receive your love without grasping, demeaning, neglecting or taking advantage of you. You need not abruptly break off relationships that do not function in a healthy manner (unless you feel it's right and choose to do so). Simply begin to give more energy to those that do. You will find that during hard times the relationships in which there is deep caring and intimacy sustain and strengthen you.

Another way to expand your family and to build your self-esteem is to begin to find ways to connect yourself to the world beyond your doorstep. Regardless of your financial position, you can give of yourself and receive the benefits of getting to know some people outside your day-to-day life. Perhaps you've always been interested in another culture and can find an organization that helps immigrants or provides relief there. Or, through your church or university or local agencies, you might get involved in helping the homeless and hungry in your own town or city. You don't need to spend a lot of time; you'd be amazed at how good you feel when you've added an occasional activity to your life that connects you with your world family.

Step 3: Learn communication skills

To survive and grow as a family unit before and during the depression requires improving our ability to work together. One of the key ingredients to successful family teamwork is communication. Each of us talks and listens for many hours every day, and most of us take it for granted. When our relationships break down, however, we often blame "a lack of communication." We are complex beings who must face the fact that the way in which we interact with others is a vital part of our health. Just as we must learn skills to effectively manage our lives and support ourselves, communication skills can be learned and can mean the difference between tragedy and triumph in difficult times. During times of crisis, we tend to feel disconnected from others. A natural reaction to failure and loss and the fear and anxiety they bring is to withdraw. However, withdrawal only makes us more miserable, and that misery consumes vital energy that could be used in productive ways. Shakespeare's Macbeth advised, "Give sorrow words: the grief that does not speak, whispers in the over-wrought heart and bids it break."

Dr. Julius Segal, author of *Winning Life's Toughest Battles* and a psychologist who has done pioneering work with prisoners of war, hostages, refugees, and Holocaust survivors, cites communication as a "lifeline for survival." He tells of POWs who found ingenious ways to communicate with each other, including tap codes, facial expressions, even belching in code! In these extreme circumstances, reaching out to another person could often mean the difference between survival and suicide. During a depression we will need to have well developed communication within our families to insure that we are able to stick together through the difficult struggles we must face.

Important elements of good family communication skills are learning how to listen and how to speak in a direct non-accusatory manner. Techniques that will foster your listening abilities include conveying acceptance through body language, listening to the feelings behind the words, "active listening" or reflecting back what the other person says, asking for clarification when you don't understand, and developing the ability to communicate your empathy and caring for the person you are listening to.

Realize that no one but you is ultimately responsible for your happiness or for fulfilling your needs. You may prefer for things to happen in a certain way, or for someone to behave in a certain manner toward you, but if they don't, you must find other ways to get your needs met.

Ask for what you need. Clarity goes a long way in preventing a build-up of resentment and misunderstanding. It may seem "selfish" or feel scary to ask for exactly what you want, but you'll find that others appreciate the opportunity to respond to your requests rather than being manipulated or blamed for not fulfilling needs they didn't know you had. When you ask for something, offer the other person a chance to express his or her feelings or concerns as well.

Learning some basic communication skills can be good psychological insurance for you, your friends and family. You might consider taking a class or workshop or having a family counselor help you learn some of these techniques. Like learning to swim, it sure does help to know how *before* you really need it!

Step 4: Start a new tradition: the family meeting

A regular, scheduled time when your family can focus on itself can be a useful and delightful addition to the week or month. It provides a forum for planning celebrations, introducing new traditions, and addressing gripes and grumbles. It ensures that family members are truly heard when they have something to say or when they want feedback, advice, or support from the family. It gives the family an opportunity to recognize achievements and special events in family members' lives. Children, especially, look forward to family meetings as a time when they can receive not only undivided attention, but a voice in decision-making and family planning. They learn much from these interactions that they will take with them into their own families in adulthood.

You can structure your family meeting in ways that meet your needs. Some families like to have formal meetings and take votes on decisions; others prefer a looser structure. A few basic guidelines can help your family meetings run smoothly and develop into an important part of your lives.

Establish some simple rules that must be followed. These can include how decisions will be made, how individuals are given "the floor" and recognized to speak, and how conflict is to be handled. Parents must be careful not to allow the family meeting to deteriorate into a lecture session in which the adults talk down to the kids and hand out new regulations or punishments.

A few guidelines that will help any family meeting stay on track include: a) No interruptions. You may have a rotating "monitor" position with the monitor making sure the rules are followed at each meeting. b) Own feelings. Those who have learned communication skills can help guide members to express themselves in terms of "I" rather than "you" or "he/she." When everybody is familiar with this way of speaking, the monitor can help members stay on track. c) End each meeting on a positive note. Perhaps a snack or a fun activity can follow each meeting. Some families like to end the meeting with a compliment session in which each member praises another with a positive statement.

Keep a running agenda for the upcoming meeting posted somewhere. Throughout the week or month, members can add items to the agenda. Everyone then gets a chance to think about it; often issues posted on the agenda are worked out in the interim and can then be erased. If there's nothing in particular to talk about, a family activity can be planned and a "good news" report delivered by each member.

Keep a family journal. This will contain the "minutes" of the family meetings, and can be kept by someone who likes to write or by someone different each time. Reading the minutes from the last meeting can be fun; years later, the journal provides a scrapbook of nostalgia that is treasured by all.

Some families like to begin and end their meetings with a prayer, a blessing or a poem, or perhaps a song or a musical selection played by one of the children. The family meeting can provide a point of stability during times of rush or crisis. It also gets members into the habit of regularly communicating with others, learning how to resolve conflicts and how to give and receive help and support. Occasionally, if larger problems, conflicts or obstacles appear, a family counselor might be brought in to help facilitate change and growth. When a family meeting is a regular part of life, getting this type of outside help is not difficult or intimidating.

The family meeting builds team spirit and helps each member to feel a special responsibility toward family solidarity. When difficult decisions must be made or lifestyle changes faced, everyone feels a part of those decisions; this sense of control can be an important part of the family's psychological well-being. The family meeting is an excellent forum for beginning to introduce the possibility of a depression coming and for everyone to work together to make plans for preparation.

Step 5: Practice shifting roles

An important part of family adaptability is the ability to shift positions and roles. This ability also contributes to individual family members' self-esteem and confidence. Often we find ourselves locked into roles, duties, and obligations for no reason other than that at some point it "just worked out that way." While we may take pride in the wonderful way we fulfil our roles and responsibilities, if we are unable to share them with others or to take on jobs and behaviors we're not accustomed to, we limit both ourselves and the people in our lives.

First, take a look at the way the family is financially supported. Is there one person responsible for all the income? Who makes the decisions about spending? Who controls the checkbook? Who makes the purchases? Are these roles fixed? How would things change if all these roles were shifted?

Next, what about household responsibilities? Who takes out the garbage? Who cooks? Who does laundry? Who maintains the car? Who takes care of the pets? Who maintains the yard, the plants, the house? Who plans holidays, vacations, and outings? Who makes sure everyone's medical and dental needs are addressed? What are the children's needs? What are their responsibilities? Who communicates with their school or day care professionals? How are decisions made about what to buy for the children? Who maintains their recreational schedules — sports, school activities, sleep-overs? How do you feel about your children working for pay? How do the children feel about taking on responsibilities such as chores and babysitting?

Many of the decisions about who does all of these important tasks are made by default rather than by conscious choice. The person doing each becomes an "expert" at his task and other family members depend on him or her. But what happens when a crisis occurs? A rigid family continues to try to maintain all of these responsibilities in the same old way. As a consequence, resentment and exhaustion begin to grow.

You can begin to increase your family's adaptability by practicing shifts in responsibility. Start small; for example, if one person *always* takes out the garbage and another *always* does the laundry, have them shift positions for awhile. You can progressively shift nearly all the responsibilities so that everyone gets a chance to meet all the family needs at one time or another. Of course, small children should not be given responsibilities they can't handle, but with a little creative thinking even little ones can participate. The result is a highly adaptable family and a boost in self-esteem for each of its members.

Diversifying family income

Diversifying your family's income now may prove invaluable when the depression comes. Many families survived and thrived during the last Depression when the children provided the primary source of income through odd jobs, bottle collecting, paper routes, snow shoveling, and babysitting. The more potential sources of income that are available, the less chance there is that there will be no family income at all during the Depression. Start thinking of ways to work together to bring in new sources of income.

MARRIAGE

During the Great Depression of the thirties the divorce rate took a sharp decline; however, over a million wives and children were abandoned by their husbands. With the recent loosening of both society's views on divorce and the laws governing it, marriages under stress are less likely than ever to remain intact. The National Commission on Mental Health and Unemployment estimates that the unemployed divorce and separate almost four times as often as others.

Marriage is no longer an institution to which we are bound throughout life. Because we can no longer take our relationships for granted, we must begin to learn and practice the skills that will help us communicate with each other, solve problems, and persevere through the difficult times. Talking and listening skills such as those previously mentioned can be learned and applied in our marriages as well; popular courses include Effectiveness Training (based on the books by Thomas Gordon) and Human Relations Training (based on psychologist Carl Rogers' work). These skills are often called "active listening" skills and are well worth the time spent to learn and practice them.

Communication within a marriage involves a deeper level of give-and-take than other relationships. The attention required is much greater and the demands upon us can be overwhelming at times. We bring all of our life experience into this primary relationship, including the role models our parents presented and experiences in adolescence that shaped our attitudes toward others. We often find ourselves at cross-purposes because of this "baggage" from the past. Our expectations of one another may be at odds; unfulfilled expectations cause stress which can overload a marriage in times of economic and social hardship.

The first step in resolving or preventing difficulties is clarity. What do you value? What do you expect? What are your priorities in your own life and in your marriage? What do you need from your spouse? When you can take an honest look at these and share them with your spouse, you can, together, begin to build the support, respect, and trust upon which a healthy relationship grows.

What do you value?

Working separately, rate the following items in importance from one (not very important) to five (of primary importance to me). When you are finished, make a list of your "fives" and your "ones." Then rank your "fives" in order of priority, and get together with your partner again.

Partner One:

_____Career, work, vocation

_____Taking spiritual or religious teachings seriously and living by them

_____Having authority, status, or influence

_____Success, achievement

_____A primary relationship

_____Having children; taking care of my children and doing things with/for them

_____Enjoying the pleasures of life; having fun

_____Being straightforward and honest with others

_____Being accepted by others

_____Taking care of my health

_____Having beautiful things and surroundings

_____Doing things for others

_____Living by ethical standards

_____Taking care of my appearance

_____Being independent; my freedom

_____Maintaining my commitments

_____Relationships with my parents and family members

_____Sexual fulfillment

_____Contributing something important to the world

_____Financial security

_____Buying and enjoying nice things

_____Having challenging experiences

_____Being different from others

_____My friendships

_____My pets

_____Following spectator sports

_____Creative and artistic endeavors

_____Preserving my family traditions and background

_____Continuing my education, growing in knowledge and skills

_____My hobbies

_____Sports; physical fitness

_____Working for social justice or political change

_____Being part of a community

"Ones" Priority List

_____

_____

_____

_____

_____

_____

"Fives" Priority List

_____

_____

_____

_____

_____

_____

Partner Two:

_____Career, work, vocation

_____Taking spiritual or religious teachings seriously and living by them

_____Having authority, status, or influence

_____Success, achievement

_____A primary relationship

_____Having children; taking care of my children and doing things with/for them

_____Enjoying the pleasures of life; having fun

_____Being straightforward and honest with others

_____Being accepted by others

_____Taking care of my health

_____Having beautiful things and surroundings

_____Doing things for others

_____Living by ethical standards

_____Taking care of my appearance

_____Taking care of my appearance

_____Being independent; my freedom

_____Maintaining my commitments

_____Relationships with my parents and family members

_____Sexual fulfillment

_____Contributing something important to the world

_____Financial security

_____Buying and enjoying nice things

_____Having challenging experiences

_____Being different from others

_____My friendships

_____My pets

_____Following spectator sports

_____Creative and artistic endeavors

_____Preserving my family traditions and background

_____Continuing my education, growing in knowledge and skills

_____My hobbies

_____Working for social justice or political change

_____Being part of a community

"Ones" Priority List

_____

_____

_____

_____

_____

_____

"Fives" Priority List

_____

_____

_____

_____

_____

_____

Now, taking turns (no interruptions!), tell each other about your top five and bottom five, and why you ranked them as such. Then, together, answer the following questions:

1. Which, if any, do you both have on your "top five" list?

2. Which, if any, do you both have on your "bottom five" list?

3. Which, if any, appeared on one partner's "top five" and the other's "bottom five" list?

4. Have each partner complete the following sentence: "From my point of view, we deal with our differing values in the following manner: (Select the appropriate response/s)

Partner 1

____We ignore our differences

____I give up mine and give yours more importance

____You give up yours and give mine more importance

____I try to get you to adopt my values

____You try to get me to adopt your values

____We talk about our differences and compromise

____Our differing values cause a lot of arguments

____We both give up our values to avoid conflict

____We never talk about our values

Partner 2

____We ignore our differences

____I give up mine and give yours more importance

____You give up yours and give mine more importance

____I try to get you to adopt my values

____You try to get me to adopt your values

____We talk about our differences and compromise

____Our differing values cause a lot of arguments

____We both give up our values to avoid conflict

____We never talk about our values

5. Complete the following sentence: "I feel _____ as a result of the way we deal with our differing values." (Examples: contented, fulfilled, frustrated, resentful, angry, grateful, agitated, happy).

6. The basic values that seem to be the foundation of our relationship are:

_____

_____

_____

7. The area in which we conflict the most is:

_____

_____

_____

8. Exchange lists. Look at your partners top five and find the values with which yours conflict, and circle them. Now complete the following sentence, finding at least one positive aspect of each of the circled values: "I appreciate your value of _____ because . . ." For example, "I appreciate your value of contributing something important to the world because it helps me to think beyond our own concerns."

9. Now, using your own list again, have each partner write down:
  a) three ways I could affirm your values while accepting our differences.
  b) three ways you could affirm my values while accepting our differences.
  For example: "I can affirm your value for friendships by not complaining when you go out with your friends. You can affirm my value for taking care of my appearance by complimenting me and noticing when I've changed my hair."

10. One way we could affirm our shared values this month would be:

_____

_____

_____

_____

Expectations

We often enter marriage with unspoken expectations about the roles we and our spouses will play. Clashing expectations can create bubbling resentments and flare into full-scale conflict during times of crisis. Our expectations can sometimes border on addictions; we expect things to be a certain way, and when they're not, we become unhappy, angry, anxious or depressed. These feelings create a snarl of negativity both in our thinking and our behavior. We hang on more tightly to our expectations and begin talking to ourselves negatively, building more and more resentment, guilt, frustration, and fear into our relationships — pushing others away and insuring that our expectations will *not* be met!

Changing our expectations to preferences is a positive step toward emotional independence and harmonious relationships. What is the difference between the following two statements?

a. "You must provide for this family!"

b. "I feel more at peace when I'm financially secure. Can we talk about ways I could deal with these feelings?"

The first statement is a demand, while the second expresses a preference and leaves a door open for the other person to get involved willingly. We are each responsible for our own feelings and preferences and for getting our own needs met. When we relinquish that responsibility, the ego (the part of us that is responsible for maintaining our psychological balance) loses its boundaries and begins to grasp at whomever is now responsible as if they are a part of the self. The other person's ego then assumes a defensive posture, for it, too, is responsible for maintaining personal balance and not losing its boundaries.

When we take responsibility for our own preferences, rather than grasping at another's sense of self, we offer an opportunity to serve. The healthy individual has a desire to serve, to help, to offer comfort and support to others. When the ego is not under attack, this desire prevails and one is much more likely to try to help others get their needs met. In marriage, more than any other relationship, the boundaries tend to blur and preferences can easily deteriorate into demands. Preventing this deterioration will make solving problems a team effort rather than a matter of blame, guilt, and avoidance.

Developing a mutually supportive relationship

Everyone needs love and support. This need is a foundation for marriage itself. When economic and social conditions become unstable, the need for nurturing, supportive love in our relationships is greater than ever. Failing to adequately support your partner during times of crisis can create serious, long-term problems that are difficult to overcome. Many people do not understand the importance of trust (built by consistent support and commitment) in a relationship until it is too late.

"Support" is a word that is used a lot in this chapter. What does it mean? It can mean different things to different people; basically, it is like a net into which your partner is not afraid to tumble. A supportive person is accepting, caring, respectful, and attentive to the other. A supportive person is willing to focus on the other at times of need and provide protection, encouragement, understanding, and a "safe place" to be vulnerable.

One person's way of offering support may not be what is needed by the other. If you can learn about one another's support needs now, you are much more likely to develop responses that can save your relationship in times of crisis. The following questions will identify the best ways to support each other:

Have each partner place a plus (+) indicating "helpful to me when I'm feeling anxious, depressed, angry, or vulnerable" or minus (-) indicating "not helpful to me" in front of each of the following:

Partner 1

_____Affection (hugs, kisses, holding my hand, giving me a massage, snuggling)

_____Cheering me up with jokes, making light of the situation

_____Teasing me

_____Telling me about similar things that happened to you

_____Telling me about people who are worse off than me

_____Being with me in silence

_____Leaving me alone

_____Telling me what to do to solve the problem

_____Listening to me lovingly, with total attention

_____Consoling me

_____Letting me know it is okay to feel the way I feel

_____Doing something for me (cook a meal, take me out, send me flowers, leave a love note somewhere for me)

_____Asking me how I got myself into the situation

_____Allowing me to talk about it as much as I need to, and listening attentively when I do

_____Ignoring the problem

_____Asking me "What's the matter?"

_____Letting me know it's okay for me to cry

_____(add your own)

Partner 2

_____Affection (hugs, kisses, holding my hand, giving me a massage, snuggling)

_____Cheering me up with jokes, making light of the situation

_____Teasing me

_____Telling me about similar things that happened to you

_____Telling me about people who are worse off than me

_____Being with me in silence

_____Leaving me alone

_____Telling me what to do to solve the problem

_____Listening to me lovingly, with total attention

_____Consoling me

_____Letting me know it is okay to feel the way I feel

_____Doing something for me (cook a meal, take me out, send me
flowers, leave a love note somewhere for me)

_____Asking me how I got myself into the situation

_____Allowing me to talk about it as much as I need to, and listen-
ing attentively when I do

_____Ignoring the problem

_____Asking me "What's the matter?"

_____Letting me know it's okay for me to cry

_____(add your own)

Exchange lists and talk about what helps each of you in times of
stress and how you can practice providing support for one another.

CHILDREN

How will a depression affect the lives of your children? When we
think "Depression," many of us have pictures in our minds of what it is
like. Usually these pictures are in black and white: it's cold outside and
everyone is dressed in tattered clothing. Children with dirty faces huddle
on the street corner, trying to warm fingers that protrude from frayed
gloves. We do not know exactly what the next depression will look like.
It will probably not resemble this imaginary photograph at all. We do
know that economic change is stressful for families, regardless of the
way in which it manifests. Parents' immediate worries usually have to
do with providing for their children's material needs. Many of us feel we
can endure most any hardship, but our children are vulnerable. When
children are accustomed to having new toys, the latest fashions, and
participating in expensive recreation, it is difficult for them to understand
when a downward adjustment must be made.

Parents worry that these adjustments will affect their children's self-
esteem and social status and thus hamper them in their long-term development. Parents who had to work during their childhood or teenage
years often want to spare their children the hardships they had to
undergo. Their own self-esteem can be affected by the feeling that they
are not adequately providing for their children.

If you can, avoid thinking that your children necessarily feel the same way about this as you. They do not. Everyone has their own feelings and attitudes. Your feelings were shaped when you were young. Your children are shaping theirs now. Let them. Then find out how *they* feel.

It turns out, in fact, that children learn more from how their parents handle situations than from what they experience or what they are told. "How we respond to the crises in our own lives will help to shape our children's response to theirs," says Dr. Julius Segal. "If we live scared, so will they."

Children have a resilience and adaptability that is often much greater than adults who are more set in their ways. Many aspects of the depression may be an adventure for our children that they are able to face with wonder and a smile. We need to give our children more credit for this ability and prepare them for engaging their special abilities in a healthy way.

We can begin to wean our children from expensive advertised toys that they see on television. A good place to start is by limiting their weekly dose of television. The values and violence of television and video games will not communicate the love and caring they will need to thrive in a time of hardship. Explain at family meetings that difficult economic times may be coming and that everyone will need to contribute their part to the family preparations. Instead of loading them down with more GI Joe's and Super Atomic Turbocharged Laseramas on holidays and birthdays, give them practical things and imaginative gifts like a certificate good for a day's hike alone with Dad, art supplies, a cookbook for children, gardening tools, lessons or a musical instrument.

An important part of preparing children for the depression is encouraging them to get interested in inexpensive forms of entertainment such as bicycling, hiking, and drawing. One of the most exciting places in your neighborhood is also one of the cheapest — your public library. A reordering of your children's priorities will help get them ready for a time of scarcity and will also help the family save money now. Besides, with real exploring and youthful enthusiasm, they will discover essential information or skills that will help sustain the entire family in its time of greatest need.

Another aspect of preparing your children for the depression is to teach them to look upon the homeless and the hungry with compassion, and not with fear. In developing a strong sense of family unity, be careful not to foster a feeling of "us against them." This will be counter productive to the feelings of love and security you are trying to instill.

During the depression, the situation will be one of "us against adversity," and the more people you are able to think of as "us," the less suffering other families will have to endure. As a family think about setting aside some time and resources to share with those in need. Working together to serve others is a dramatic demonstration of the strength of your family and more than anything will prepare your children and you for the depression.

Once the depression comes, for many families it may be too late to develop the skills and strength they need to see them through. Begin now to strengthen all your family relationships before the pressures of economic chaos swirl around your heads. Investing in those closest to you by learning to support one another through communication, planning, and love will reap the most important rewards of your life.

Chapter
11
Community Preparation

When the depression comes, the more people with whom we have a relationship of mutual interdependence, the more emotionally and financially secure we will be. This chapter describes ways to broaden and clarify these mutually interdependent relationships through community networks and projects.

Initiating this process of community building now will give you a solid base from which to build the support you, your family, and your community will require. Start now. Do not wait for the worst of hard times to descend. Developing a support network will take time. Later you may have to concentrate on basic survival.

The adversity of a depression tends to cause people to either become alienated and retreat from society or band together to help one another get through the common struggle. The latter course is recommended for many reasons. There is much greater emotional and material security in a mutually supportive group than there is in an individual person or family. Sharing troubles means sharing solutions to those troubles. To be truly human and a member of society entails a commitment to fellow humans. Heading for the hills with guns and canned goods may mean survival, but at what cost? A life of fear protecting your island against the tidal wave may put food in your belly, but your soul will wither and die. Lastly, since greed and the protection of narrow self-interests is helping to cause the coming depression, an escalation of such thinking will deepen and prolong the misery.

Joining with others for mutual support and self-help project development will increase your ability to survive and will also lead to invaluable emotional security. Knowing that you have friends, neighbors, and fellow community members to call on or respond to will lighten your individual burden.

A story is told of a land where the people died of starvation because they were afflicted with a malady that prevented them from bending their arms and were unable to feed themselves. They did not discover how easy it would be to eat if they fed each other. Prepare now to learn to feed each other rather than desperately trying to feed yourself when it becomes impossible.

ASSESSING AND DEVELOPING YOUR COMMUNITY SUPPORT NETWORK

Look first to the formal and informal community networks and organizations to which you already belong. Mark them here:

Level of Relationship	Superficial	Meaningful
❑ Religious or spiritual organization	_____	_____
❑ Social club	_____	_____
❑ Business or trade association	_____	_____
❑ Athletic organization or health club	_____	_____
❑ Computer user's group	_____	_____
❑ Regular class or training program	_____	_____
❑ Car pool	_____	_____
❑ Regular card game	_____	_____
❑ Community service and/or volunteer organization	_____	_____
❑ Arts or crafts group	_____	_____
❑ Emotional support group	_____	_____
❑ Group therapy	_____	_____
❑ Hobby group or club	_____	_____
❑ Veteran's group	_____	_____
❑ Alumni group	_____	_____
❑ Military reserve group	_____	_____
❑ Food cooperative or buying club	_____	_____
❑ Labor union	_____	_____
❑ Circle of friends or neighbors	_____	_____
❑ Choir or musical group	_____	_____

❏ Involvement with youth such as scouts, PTA, child care coop, coaching, etc.   _____ _____

❏ Homeowner's or Condo Association   _____ _____

❏ Political party or interest group   _____ _____

❏ Co-workers   _____ _____

❏ Neighborhood association   _____ _____

Fill in your own:

❏ _____ _____ _____

❏ _____ _____ _____

❏ _____ _____ _____

Developing meaningful relationships

When you are finished listing the networks you are involved with, go through your list and check how meaningful you consider the relationships. Meaningful relationships will help see you through the depression. Think about which of the superficial relationships you can or wish to improve. Relationships need nurturing to deepen. Going to an occasional meeting will not lead to the type of relationships necessary during hard times. Identify and list networks and individuals that you can more fully develop:

_____

_____

_____

_____

_____

Consciously examine and evaluate your community ties. Deepening existing ties comes next. If you discover you don't have many community ties that can be deepened, then work on developing them. Get involved, taking the attitude that not only will it make you more well rounded, but it is a lifeline to your future emotional and material survival.

Some suggestions on how to build deeper relationships include:
1. Invite a friend or a key individual in a group to share a meal.
2. In group and individual settings, get in the habit of sharing more about who you really are.
3. Find a common interest to build upon.
4. Bring up stimulating and thought provoking topics that may be slightly uncomfortable, rather than keeping everything light and non-controversial, i.e. the weather, sports, your children's success. Take a risk in the hope of deepening a relationship.
5. Let a person or group know that you really care and that they are an important part of your life.
6. Spend time with people outside of the setting that you usually interact with them. Schedule a weekend retreat or camping trip. You may discover very different sides of each other.
7. Share an intense experience together like an Outward Bound program or a personal growth seminar. This helps a group to bond more quickly and come closer together.

COMMUNITY SUPPORT AND THE DEPRESSION

As you develop your community support network, you are laying the groundwork for what will become your depression support network. The process of turning what may be loose connections with a myriad of groups and people into a positive force for banding together during a depression requires planning and effort. A key element to keep in mind is that real community support and strength grows out of action and working together. A philosophical or emotional commitment to community will not suffice when hard times come.

The practical steps your group's plan for action entails will vary according to each situation and needs, but here are some suggestions on how to begin the process:
1. Plan personal and family needs using the charts in the previous chapters. Then ask, do you intend to look to the community for emotional and material support? Will your own preparation allow you to help others? What kind of support can you give and receive?
2. Does your current network adequately provide the support your family is likely to need during the depression? Does your network have the strength to withstand the ravages of hard economic times?
3. Which needs will your current support network be unable to meet? What community needs are currently not being met and will become bigger problems in the depression?

Actively developing support connections

Talk to a group you already belong to about the coming economic hard times (in some areas the hard times have already come) and what you can do together to help each other and the community. For example, a natural place to initiate this is in your church or spiritual organization. Talk to fellow church members about what the response of the congregation will be to the potential suffering of members. Set up a social assistance fund or expand one already in place to help see member families through the depression. Additionally, the church may decide to expand the scope of its community mission work to feed, cloth, and house more needy people. The church may decide to set up a variety of self-help projects to assist its members and others in need.

Remember the principle of inclusiveness will nurture souls — both yours and the ones you include — much more than exclusiveness will.

If the group shows little interest in the process, consider forming or joining a group focused on depression preparation. Ask individuals you know from your various community networks to join the effort. You may have to sell them on the idea. Give them a copy of this book and ask them to read it and share their reactions with you. As the depression becomes a reality for more people, you will have to do less convincing.

Have your established group or your new group make concrete plans of action. Brainstorm possible areas where you all can have an impact. Weed out the impractical ideas, and select the top priorities for action. Once you establish priorities, develop step by step plans for how to accomplish the priorities. Make sure that you set deadlines and specific responsibilities for individuals to insure proper follow through. Possible projects your group can undertake will be detailed later in the chapter. Once your group learns to work together on a mutual support project, the possibilities for success will greatly increase.

The types of projects are limited only by the resources available and your imagination. As you experience success, think about expanding your group to work with other groups, thus expanding the base of skills and resources. This will enable you to help many more people. A community consisting of many such expanding and interacting concentric circles will have the emotional and material strength to greatly lessen the hardships faced by its members.

Depressions and self-help

Hard times foster innovative solutions to social and economic problems. In the depressions of the 1890's and the 1930's, many self-help projects sprang up and flourished. Community gardens, cooperatives, and labor exchanges surged as people found little help in traditional economic structures. Corporate America laid off millions, and some of them turned to themselves and their communities for answers. Some of the alternative institutions developed during depressions remain today, but the majority faded away when economic conditions improved and traditional jobs became available. Looking at self-help projects of the past and developing new ideas is a good place for your mutual support group to start the process of selecting action-oriented projects.

COMMUNITY PROJECTS

Community gardens

Community gardens grow food on land used in common by individuals and groups. Although during a depression it is unrealistic to expect to feed all the hungry from such gardens, many people benefit from participation in growing their own food. The benefits include the obvious one of producing food, and the less obvious ones of bringing people closer to each other and to nature. In our society where children conceive of their daily food as something that comes from the supermarket wrapped in plastic or contained within a brightly colored box, putting our hands in the soil and nurturing seedlings to maturity is a tremendously life affirming process.

The concept of community gardens is an ancient one that predates our current system of private property and fenced in farmland by thousands of years. From the first evolution of human beings from hunters and gatherers to cultivators and farmers, land was held in common stewardship to produce food for the whole community. As recently as the middle ages in England, all land surrounding a village was farmed together in an open field system.

Growing population necessitated change, and in 1709, Parliament passed the first law that mandated fenced fields and closed commons. However, in the early 19th century, all English cities and towns were required by law to make garden space available for the poor and unemployed.[1] This practice spread throughout Europe and became known as the allotment garden system; it successfully continues to operate today.

The first widespread development of community gardens in the United States was initiated by the progressive mayor of Detroit, Hazen Pingree. In the depression of the 1890's, the industry dependent city of Detroit was ravaged. Commenting in June of 1894 as he started the program, Pingree said, "The destitution of many of the inhabitants of Detroit is well known, and the outlook for them the coming winter to procure food to keep body and soul together is gloomy in the extreme."[2] To relieve some of the suffering, Pingree personally developed a comprehensive system of community gardens on unused city and private land. Detroit's system became extremely successful and spread to cities throughout the United States. The program came to be known as Pingree's Potato Patch.[3]

Pingree helped establish an American tradition of community gardens that is periodically revived in times of economic and martial strife. World War I saw thousands of Liberty Gardens, the Great Depression of the 1930's brought extensive community gardening, and World War II brought millions of Victory Gardens. At the height of the Victory Gardens project an estimated 40 million people were involved.[4]

Starting a community garden

Starting a community garden now will give you experience before the depression and will improve the richness and fertility of the soil. If your group decides to start a community garden, research what is already available. Many U.S. cities today have ongoing community garden programs. Assistance is often provided through county agricultural extension offices and municipal parks and recreation departments. Often land, seeds, and tools can be obtained for free or at low cost.

Key components of a successful community garden include structure, personnel, site, soil, gardening expertise, finances, pest control, and distribution of produce. For an overview of these topics consult a book such as Jamie Jobb's *The Complete Book of Community Gardening*. For more specific information on gardening topics, check your local library or bookstore for a selection of hundreds of books. In addition, there are dozens of magazines that have the most up-to-date information on the latest developments in gardening.

For the purpose of your depression preparation, consider the following: Does a member of your group have a large garden space that could be more productive if you all pitch in? Who among your group is the most experienced in gardening? Is there a vacant lot in your neighborhood that would make a good site for a community garden? Are facilities available for canning, freezing, or storing produce?

Growing a garden together is one of the simplest ways of developing a closer knit group that will be better able to tackle more ambitious group projects. The many and diverse tasks you need to accomplish give scope for the talents and resources of each member to manifest. You will observe the strengths and weaknesses of your group through their actions. In addition, the tangible results of your harvest provide great encouragement and give a tasty success to build upon.

Cooperatives

Cooperatives are enterprises that involve a group of people working together for mutual self-interest. Cooperatives differ from traditional businesses in that the goal is to provide quality goods and services to the membership at the lowest possible cost, not to make a monetary profit. They are people centered, not profit centered. The two basic types of cooperatives are producer's cooperatives, such as farmer's and manufacturer's; and consumer's cooperatives including food, housing, health care, day care, and credit unions. The number of cooperatives increases dramatically in depressions as individuals pool their limited resources for mutual benefit and survival.

Today's cooperative movement has its roots in England in 1844. A group of 28 weavers in Rochdale, weary of slave labor conditions, staged an unsuccessful wildcat strike. Their strike failed, but out of their struggle they created the first successful modern cooperative. Their venture attracted so much interest in a time of extreme exploitation that it eventually expanded to include 30,000 members and 75 stores. The fundamental principles they developed have guided cooperatives ever since. In modified form they are:

1. Open membership. Membership is voluntary, without discrimination of any kind, and open to anyone who can use the services of the co-op. Membership is subject only to good faith and acceptance of member responsibilities.
2. Democratic control, or one member, one vote. Administrators are elected or appointed by members and accountable to them. Voting by proxy is limited in most cooperatives.
3. Limited or no return on equity capital.
4. The net surplus belongs to the user-owners: either the net savings are distributed to the members, or the members agree to use the surplus for their mutual benefit or that of the community.
5. Continuous education, not only of members, but also informing the community and the public about cooperatives and promoting consumer education generally.

(from Rodney S. Wead, *The Neighborhood Cooperative*, 1983, reprinted with permission.)

After Rochdale, cooperatives expanded rapidly throughout England and the rest of the world. Scandinavia, in particular, embraced cooperatives. Today over one-third of all retail business in Sweden is through cooperatives, including over half of all food purchases. In North America cooperatives have primarily taken hold among farmers, both with production and consumption. In Canada, 80 per cent of all grain business and 50 per cent of dairy products are handled by cooperatives.[5] In the United States, five of every six farmers belong to at least one co-op.

Popular brands, including Sunkist, Ocean Spray, Land 'o Lakes, Diamond Walnuts, and Sunsweet, are products of farmer-owned cooperatives. There is some debate as to whether the large producer's cooperatives fully follow the Rochdale principles and should be categorized as true cooperatives.

Consumer's cooperatives took much longer to take hold in the United

States, and they make up only a small fraction of total retail trade. The largest upsurges in consumer's cooperatives have come in times of turmoil. Just as with community gardens, hard times force people to get together and consider new ways of doing things. Joseph Warbasse, then president of the Cooperative League, wrote the following in 1923.

Born in poverty, adversity encourages (the cooperative movement). When the dominant system oppresses society with injustices and war, the people turn to themselves for relief.[6]

Prior to the depression of the 1890's, most cooperatives were started by immigrants from Europe, with Finns responsible for over 60% of U.S. cooperatives. During the 1890's, hundreds of cooperative self-help enterprises grew. Many of them went under as economic conditions improved.

The Depression of the 1930's also saw the growth of cooperatives in many areas of life. The movement gained so many adherents that Roosevelt's New Deal set up a Division of Self-Help Cooperatives under the Federal Emergency Relief Act (FERA). This provided capital that was instrumental in starting thousands of cooperative ventures as an integral part of government relief efforts. The most successful co-ops included the people served as essential to the management and administration of the project. Attempts by the government to arbitrarily create cooperatives in name only were failures.[7]

Many churches started cooperatives during the Depression. This was objected to by some church-going businessmen who viewed it as unfair competition and "creeping communism." However, others such as the successful Boston businessman Edward Filene fully supported the movement. He gave the following address to the synod of New York of the Presbyterian church in October of 1936.

The cooperative movement, to be sure, is basically economic, as was the family and other institutions which have made it possible for man to realize so many of his spiritual ideals. But it is more than economic. It is charged with aspiration and with idealism. It is warmly, humanly passionate; and it is demonstrating day by day that there is more real satisfaction and more business success in working together for the common good than there ever could be in a free-for-all struggle on the part of everybody to get ahead of everybody else. And many churches, I am glad to say, of many faiths and creeds, are already helping to organize such cooperation.[8]

Perhaps the most successful type of cooperatives that came out of the last depression were credit unions. The Federal Credit Union Act was passed in June 1934, and the next six years helped credit unions surge from a total of 2,489 with a membership of 427,097 to 9,023 with a membership of 2,826,612. Today there are 16,193 U.S. credit unions with a membership of 57.6 million. The total assets are $183.6 billion dollars.

Cooperatives in the United States declined with the end of the Depression and World War II. The movement was revitalized in the late 1960's and early 1970's, partly as a result of increased political dissent among young people. Thousands of small and larger cooperatives sprang up in every city. These were mainly consumer's food cooperatives that were often loosely structured and poorly managed. Many have closed, but those with better management remain today.

Cities that have shown particular success with cooperatives in the last 20 years include Minneapolis/St. Paul, Seattle, Madison, and Boston. Large thriving co-ops include the Berkeley Co-op in California, Recreational Equipment Incorporated (REI), now in several states, and the Greenbelt Co-op in the Potomac area. Greenbelt has over 50,000 members and includes furniture, supermarket, and auto service divisions.

There are many thriving low income cooperatives. Rodney Wead in his excellent book, *The Neighborhood Cooperative*, describes some particularly successful cooperative ventures including the Bethel Housing Co-op on Chicago's west side. Through sweat equity (where through the tenants' labor they become owners), they have grown to the point of having fifty apartment units and complementary food and sewing cooperatives.

A misconception about cooperatives is that they are socialist in nature. Cooperatives differ from classical socialism in that the ownership of a cooperative lies with its members, not with the government. As self-help projects, cooperatives show people at their best: working together to help their fellow members and themselves. Other than some possible start up assistance, cooperatives operate independently and successfully without any assistance from the government or corporations.

Starting a cooperative

The most successful cooperatives start from the ground up when potential members feel that their needs can be better served by their own efforts. As we have seen in other areas of life, taking control is an essential part of preparing for the depression. Joining existing cooperatives and forming new ones will help you take control of your economic life.

Your mutual support group may decide to undertake starting a cooperative as a self-help depression preparation project. The simplest form of cooperative is a food buying club, where you all buy food collectively and divide it by households, thus getting wholesale prices and insuring higher quality. You can start a food buying club with as few as five families. Twenty five families is usually recommended as the maximum size for such an endeavor. If the club becomes larger, you lose some of the

feeling of togetherness and add bureaucracy that saves you little money
or time. If a club grows larger, it may consider splitting into
two or joining with other food buying clubs to form a
store front cooperative.

Housing cooperatives are a natural answer to the
urban blight that has left many cities with abandoned
and neglected buildings. Get together with people in
your neighborhood and approach the city or county
authorities about the possibility of turning some
unused property into productive use. Check with the
county clerk or assessor's office to find out who owns
vacant buildings. In a time of falling real estate
prices, the owner may be glad to rid him or herself of
negative cash flow as a donation or for a modest price. Many abandoned properties have probably reverted back to banks who have little
use or plans for them. Approach them about improving their community
relations by helping to make a housing cooperative a success.

Day care cooperatives are also relatively easy to start. They can begin
with parents trading off taking care of children. Often this type of cooperative can expand into a cooperative day care center where parents are
active participants in the running of the center, although there is usually
a paid staff. Several communities have co-ops such as bakeries, hard-
ware stores, auto repair shops, art galleries, and restaurants.

Your group needs to assess the skills of its members and decide what
type of cooperative best matches the skills, resources, and energy you
have available. Some of the more ambitious types of projects may be
difficult to start while most of you are working. But now you can lay the
framework for a time when many of you may have more free time than
you want. Cooperatives provide fulfilling work and incentive for the
jobless. The feeling of working for yourselves will nourish and sustain
you. Cooperatives bring hope and lessen despair.

In thinking of starting a cooperative, keep in mind that in a cooperative no one person is in charge. You are all in charge. Developing
cooperating consciousness is essential to your success. Those who are
used to working primarily in hierarchical environments will have to
adjust to the collective control of a co-op. Try to get experience working
together on small projects to build your sense of cooperation. Visit existing cooperatives to learn how they operate. Study and educate yourselves on the history and management of cooperatives. The less mis-
takes of previous cooperatives you repeat, the more successful you will
be.

Labor exchange/barter

Another important form of self-help involves the exchange of labor
and goods. In times of scarce money these types of transactions abound,
both formally and informally. The basic principle is that you have a

surplus in one area of your life and a shortage elsewhere. So you find someone who has what you need and who wants something you have a surplus of; you trade. That is called bartering.

Formal labor exchanges and barter systems give credit for goods and services you provide and debit(charge) for those that you use. The units of credit and debit are mutually decided upon by the members. Thus you do not have to find a one-to-one match with another person who has the complementary need and abundance to yours. For example, suppose Henry is skilled in auto mechanics. He provides five hours of work on member Susan's car and receives five units of credit. With his five units, he purchases some used gardening tools that had been credited to the account of Mary who no longer needed them.

The first recorded formal system of labor exchange was started in 1889 by G.D. Bernardi. He felt that labor exchanges were preferable to cooperatives, because the poor and unemployed lack the money to make purchases at cooperative stores. At first Bernardi's ideas attracted little interest, but the economic decline of the 1890's brought many people to join. By the end of the depression in 1897, 325 branch labor exchanges counted over 15,000 members. Bernardi and some of his followers saw the labor exchange as a more humane alternative to the prevailing system. As the depression waned and the country returned to business as usual, the labor exchanges faded away. Barter was common in the depression of the 1930's. Scenes of sacks of potatoes being exchanged for haircuts and gallons of milk for clothes were frequent.

Setting up a system for the exchange of labor and goods among your support group or community requires little initial effort. It can start out as simple as a card box or bulletin board that lists each persons skills, needs, and excess goods. As it develops, a newsletter can be distributed that details what is available and what people need. A more sophisticated system may use a computer to track member's accounts and to match labor and goods. If the exchange grows further, inexpensive office space may become necessary or it can be housed at a local food co-op.

Money represents a unit of measurement that is mutually agreed upon to be worth something. When many people find themselves without these agreed upon units, it is only natural to return to a system that existed long before the development of coins and paper money. Labor exchange and barter are opportunities for the jobless and poor to take control of their lives, irrespective of jobs that may or may not be available with corporations.

Other community self-help possibilities

The opportunities for working together to help one another and the wider community are many and varied. Examples of possibilities include the sharing of a common vehicle or major appliances between a few families. Everyone on the block need not own a lawn mower to use it once a week. It may be practical for members of your support group to move to the same neighborhood to facilitate sharing of tools, cars, and child care. Some groups get together to buy large quantities of food and store it safely.

If you have friends who are Mormons, invite them to speak to your group. Mormons have a long history of effective self-help projects including extensive food storage. Your group might want to visit shelters for the homeless and volunteer to help by providing food or clothes. Besides the help you provide, you will learn a lot about providing for people's needs and the strengths of your group. Contact the Mennonites, a religious group that has a great deal of valuable experience in self-help projects, frugality, and community service. In all your plans to work together, remember the principle of synergy — where the whole is more than the sum of its parts — and make it work for you.

Endnotes

1. Jamie Jobb, *The Complete Book of Community Gardening,* (New York: William Morrow, 1979), p. 72.
2. Roger Grant, *Self-Help in the 1890's Depression,* (Ames: Iowa State University Press, 1983), p. 26.
3. Grant, p. 29.
4. Jobb, p. 73.
5. Albert Lee, *How to Save Money Through Group Buying,* (New York: Stein and Day, 1977), p. 3.
6. James Warbasse, *Cooperative Democracy,* (New York: MacMillan, 1923), p. 14.
7. Joseph G. Knapp, *The Advance of American Cooperative Enterprise: 1920—1945,* (Danville: Interstate, 1973), p. 316.
8. Samuel C. Kincheloe, *Research Memorandum on Religion in the Depression,* (New York: Arno Press, 1972), p. 115.

Chapter
12
Putting it All Together

The coming depression will be a time of suffering, confusion, and despair on one hand; and positive change, opportunity, and hope on the other. We face immense but not insurmountable challenges as individuals and as a society. The choices and changes we make now will determine how much our families and communities suffer. The human capacity to adapt and adjust gives cause for optimism. Not only will the large majority survive the depression, but our world can be a better place to live after the personal and societal change brought on by the depression.

How is this possible? What good can come out of global economic turmoil? A reordering of our priorities is essential to the future survival of millions of people as well as our planet. To the extent that the depression accelerates this vital process it will be an undeniable catalyst for human progress. In the same way, the threat of a depression can be the catalyst for positive personal change.

The many areas covered in this book are all worthy of your consideration for changes. Examine your lists from previous chapters and take a look at where you can most effectively make a positive lasting change. The main areas are Financial, Career, Lifestyle, Family, Community and Inner Development, shown below:

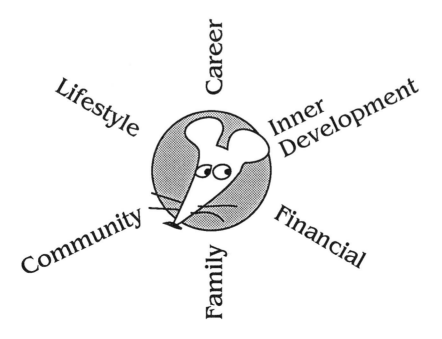

The more comprehensive your preparation is, the better able you will be to respond to whatever challenges the depression brings to your family. Realistically, it will be extremely difficult to work on all six areas of your life at the same time. Taking on too much at once can be overwhelming and cause you to throw up your hands in frustration and do nothing. At that point you will be left to wait with increasing anxiety as the depression slowly marches to your door. So rather than set out an impossible task for yourself, you need to develop a step by step realistic plan of action. To facilitate this process and help you prioritize, let's look at each of the six areas and evaluate your current situation. Throughout this section, pay special attention to the questions marked with a check (✔).

An example of how to use the process follows the charts, on page 169.

FINANCIAL

1. To evaluate your financial situation and your needs, go back to Chapter 5 (page 48) and plug in the figure for your current liquid assets:

_____

2. On a scale of 1 to 5 with 1 being the least secure and 5 the most secure, rate how secure these assets are:

1   2   3   4   5

A rating of 1 or 2 rates a ✔.

3. Fill in your survival figure from page (47):

_____

4. Subtract the figure from question 3 from the figure from question 1.

_____ ✔

If this amount is greater than you can likely accumulate with your current income and rate of savings and investments, you need to make increasing your income and/or decreasing your expenses a high priority.

CAREER

1. Review the list of careers that are likely to be more secure during the depression. Is your profession on this list or related to a field with potential for growth?

   YES _____   NO_____   If no ✔

2. Review the list of careers that are likely to be less secure during the depression. Is your profession on this list or related to a field that will be declining?

YES_____ NO_____ If yes ✔

3. Taking into consideration the above questions and your individual situation including factors of union contracts, length of employment, financial situation of your company and industry, etc. rate how secure your job will be in the event of a depression. Use a scale of 1 to 5 with 1 being the least secure and 5 the most secure:

1   2   3   4   5

A rating of 1 or 2 rates a ✔

LIFESTYLE

Review the lifestyle chapter and answer the following questions:

1. On a scale of 1 to 5 with 1 being the least important and 5 being the most important, rate how important you feel simplifying your life is to your preparation for the depression:

1   2   3   4   5

A rating of 4 or 5 rates a ✔

2. On a scale of 1 to 5 with 1 being the least important and 5 being the most important, rate how important you feel growing beyond materialism is to your preparation for the depression:

1   2   3   4   5

A rating of 4 or 5 rates a ✔

3. On a scale of 1 to 5 with 1 being the least important and 5 being the most important, rate how important you feel increasing your self-esteem is to your preparation for the depression:

1   2   3   4   5

A rating of 4 or 5 rates a ✔

4. On a scale of 1 to 5 with 1 being the least important and 5 being the most important, rate how important you feel improving your diet is to your preparation for the depression:

1   2   3   4   5

A rating of 4 or 5 rates a ✔

5. On a scale of 1 to 5 with 1 being the least important and 5 being the most important, rate how important you feel increasing your fitness is to your preparation for the depression:

1   2   3   4   5

A rating of 4 or 5 rates a ✔

6. On a scale of 1 to 5 with 1 being the least important and 5 being the most important, rate how important you feel bringing more humor into your life is to your preparation for the depression:
1   2   3   4   5
A rating of 4 or 5 rates a ✔

7. On a scale of 1 to 5 with 1 being the least important and 5 being the most important, rate how important you feel improving your stress management is to your preparation for the depression:
1   2   3   4   5
A rating of 4 or 5 rates a ✔

INNER DEVELOPMENT

Review the chapter on inner development and answer the following questions:

1. On a scale of 1 to 5 with 1 being the least satisfied and 5 being the most satisfied, rate how satisfied you are with the harmony between your guiding principles and your actions:
1   2   3   4   5
A rating of 1 or 2 rates a ✔

2. On a scale of 1 to 5 with 1 being the least important and 5 being the most important, rate how important you feel your inner development is to your preparation for the depression:
1   2   3   4   5
A rating of 4 or 5 rates a ✔

FAMILY

Review the chapter on the family and answer the following questions:

1. On a scale of 1 to 5 with 1 being the weakest and 5 being the strongest, rate how strong you feel your family safety net is:
1   2   3   4   5
A rating of 1 or 2 rates a ✔

2. On a scale of 1 to 5 with 1 being the least effective and 5 being the most effective, rate the effectiveness of your family's communication:
1   2   3   4   5
A rating of 1 or 2 rates a ✔

3. On a scale of 1 to 5 with 1 being the least adaptable and 5 being the most adaptable, rate how well you think your family will adapt to the challenges a depression will bring:
1   2   3   4   5
A rating of 1 or 2 rates a ✔

4. On a scale of 1 to 5 with 1 being the least prepared and 5 being the most prepared, rate how well prepared your children are for a depression:

1   2   3   4   5

A rating of 1 or 2 rates a ✔

COMMUNITY

Review the chapter on community preparation and answer the following questions:

1. On a scale of 1 to 5 with 1 being the least extensive and 5 being the most extensive, rate the extent of your community connections:

1   2   3   4   5

A rating of 1 or 2 rates a ✔

2. On a scale of 1 to 5 with 1 being the least important and 5 being the most important, rate how important you feel developing a community support network is to your preparation for the depression:

1   2   3   4   5

A rating of 1 or 2 rates a ✔

3. On a scale of 1 to 5 with 1 being the least important and 5 the most important, rate how important you feel developing community projects such as cooperatives, community gardens, and barter/labor exchanges are to your preparation for the depression:

1   2   3   4   5

A rating of 4 or 5 rates a ✔

SETTING PRIORITIES

Now that you have taken a look at each of the six main areas, you should have a good idea of problem areas that need your attention. The following steps will help you to prioritize the areas of concern:

1. Synthesize the items that need special attention by listing below all the items that have a check next to them:

Area of Concern   **Priority Level**

_____   _____

_____   _____

_____   _____

_____   _____

_____   _____

_____ _____

_____ _____

_____ _____

2. Read over your whole list; then determine what level of priority to assign to each item. Assign an **A** to areas that need immediate attention (within the next three months), **B** to areas that you will address later (within six months to one year), and **C** to areas you will address only once you make significant progress on your **A** and **B** list.

3. Take all the **A**-priority areas and list them below then rank them in order of importance:

A-Priority Areas of Concern   **Rank**

_____ _____

_____ _____

_____ _____

_____ _____

_____ _____

_____ _____

PLAN OF ACTION

Now you have your list in order of importance of the areas that need your immediate attention for preparation. Take each of these priority areas and develop a plan of action for what steps you will take to address these areas of concern.

Priority One (most important from your **A**-priority list)

Area of concern:

_____

Action steps:
I will complete the following task: By the following date:

1. _____   _____

2. _____   _____

3. _____   _____

4. _____ _____

5. _____ _____

Priority Two (second most important from your **A**-priority list)

Area of concern:

_____

Action steps:
I will complete the following task: By the following date:

1. _____ _____

2. _____ _____

3. _____ _____

4. _____ _____

5. _____ _____

Priority Three (third most important from your **A**-priority list)

Area of concern:

_____

Action steps:
I will complete the following task: By the following date:

1. _____ _____

2. _____ _____

3. _____ _____

4. _____ _____

5. _____ _____

Priority Four (fourth most important from your **A**-priority list)
Area of concern:

_____

Action steps:
I will complete the following task: By the following date:

1. _____   _____

2. _____   _____

3. _____   _____

4. _____   _____

5. _____   _____

Priority Five (fifth most important from your **A**-priority list)

Area of concern:

_____

Action steps:
I will complete the following task: By the following date:

1. _____   _____

2. _____   _____

3. _____   _____

4. _____   _____

5. _____   _____

In order to get an overview of all of the tasks you have set out for yourself, create a master list of all the action steps in chronological order. Then review your master list to make sure it is realistic and the tasks can be completed in the time allowed.

ACTION STEPS MASTER LIST

Task   **Target Date**

_____   _____

_____   _____

_____   _____

_____   _____

_____   _____

_____   _____

_____   _____

_____   _____

_____   _____

_____   _____

_____   _____

_____   _____

The same process can be followed for your **B** and **C** priority lists.

EXAMPLE OF SETTING PRIORITIES AND DEVELOPING A PLAN OF ACTION:

The following example will provide you with a model for your own lists:

1. Synthesis of items with checks that need special attention with an assigned priority level:

Area of Concern	Priority Level
Financial: $15,000 difference between assets and survival figure	*A*
Career: My job is on the list of jobs that will decline in the depression	*A*
Lifestyle: Simplifying my life rates a 4 in importance	*B*
Lifestyle: Increasing my fitness rates a 5 in importance	*A*
Lifestyle: Increasing my ability to handle stress rates a 5	*B*
Family: Strength of safety net rates a 1	*B*
Family: My family's communication effectiveness rates a 2	*C*
Community: Developing community projects rates a 4	*C*
Inner Development: Inner development rates a 5 in importance	*A*

2. A-priority areas listed and ranked:

A-Priority Areas of Concern	Rank
Financial: $15,000 difference between assets and survival figure	1
Career: My job is on the list of jobs that will decline in the depression	2
Lifestyle: Increasing my fitness rates a 5 in importance	4
Inner Development: Inner development rates a 5 in importance	3

PLAN OF ACTION

Priority One (most important from your **A** priority list)

Area of Concern:
Financial: $15,000 difference between assets and survival figure.

Action steps:
I will complete the following task: By the following date:

1. *Develop a tight family budget and stick to it*	*January 1*
2. *Ask my boss for a raise*	*February 1*
3. *Have my daughter start a paper route*	*March 1*
4. *Get a part time job*	*March 15*
5. *Sell cabin in the mountains*	*April 15*

Priority Two

Area of concern:
Career: My job is on the list of jobs that will decline in the depression.

Action steps:
I will complete the following task: By the following date:

1. *Write and print a new resume*	*January 15*
2. *Send out 10 resumes with cover letters to prospective employers*	*February 1*
3. *Get catalogues and applications from schools*	*February 15*
4. *Check with friends and acquaintances about job possibilities*	*March 15*
5. *Decide on possible attendance at night school and apply*	*April 1*

Priority Three

Area of concern:
Inner Development: Inner development rates a 5 in importance.

Action steps:
I will complete the following task: By the following date:

1. *Sign up for a class in meditation*   March 15

2. *Begin daily practice of meditation*   May 1

3. *Join a weekly meditation group*   June 1

Priority Four

Area of concern:
Lifestyle: Increasing my fitness rates a 5 in importance.

Action steps:
I will complete the following task: By the following date:

1. *See a doctor for a complete physical exam*   March 15

2. *Make a plan for regular exercise program*   April 1

3. *Implement plan and start*   April 10

4. *Review state of fitness and modify plan*   June 15

ACTION STEPS MASTER LIST

Task	**Target Date**
1. *Develop a tight family budget and stick to it*	*January 1*
2. *Write and print a new resume*	*January 15*
3. *Ask my boss for a raise*	*February 1*
4. *Send out 10 resumes with cover letters to prospective employers*	*February 1*
5. *Get catalogues and applications from schools*	*February 15*
6. *Check with friends and acquaintances about jobs*	*March 1*
7. *Have my daughter start a paper route*	*March 1*
8. *Get a part time job*	*March 15*

9.	*Sign up for a class in meditation*	*March 15*
10.	*See a doctor for a complete physical exam*	*March 15*
11.	*Make a plan for regular exercise program*	*April 1*
12.	*Decide on possible attendance at night school and apply*	*April 1*
13.	*Implement exercise plan and start*	*April 10*
14.	*Sell cabin in the mountains*	*April 15*
15.	*Begin daily practice of meditation*	*May 1*
16.	*Join a weekly meditation group*	*June 1*
17.	*Review state of fitness and modify plan*	*June 15*

WHERE DO YOU GO FROM HERE?

Implementing your action plan and making positive changes gives you the opportunity to face the challenges of the coming depression armed with strength and an expanding array of coping tools.

A positive approach to the depression will lighten your load and will spread that light all around you. Sharing your problems and your loving concern with others increases the possibility of creative and cooperative solutions. You will get the most benefit from this book by sharing it with others. Bring your family and friends into a discussion of the probability of a depression and the concrete positive actions you can take to deal with it.

Author's Note

I would like to hear your reactions to the book and the creative solutions you come up with. I will incorporate your suggestions into future editions of this book and into a newsletter. By learning and working together, we can speed the evolution of our world to one in which the suffering of all is lessened. Write to me at the following address:

Mark Friedman
P.O. Box 27663
Denver, CO 80227

Resources

On the inevitability of the next depression:

Batra, Ravi. *The Great Depression of 1990.* Simon and Schuster.

King, John L. *How to Profit from the Next Great Depression.* New American Library.

Malabre, Alfred L. *Beyond Our Means.* Random House.

Malkin, Lawrence. *The National Debt.* Henry Holt.

On previous depressions:

Chandler, Lester V. *America's Greatest Depression 1929-1941.* Harper and Row.

Garraty, John A. *The Great Depression.* Harcourt, Brace, Jovanovich.

Galbraith, John Kenneth. *The Great Crash.* Houghton Mifflin.

Kindleberger, Charles. *Manias, Panics, and Crashes: A History of Financial Crises.* Basic Books.

McElvaine, Robert S. *Down and Out in the Great Depression.* University of North Carolina Press.

Terkel, Studs. *Hard Times: An Oral History of the Great Depression.* Pantheon.

Westin, Jeanne. *Making Do: How Women Survived the 30's.* Follett.

On saving and budgeting:

Elgin, Duane. *Voluntary Simplicity: Toward a Way of Life that is Outwardly Simple, Inwardly Rich.* William Morrow.

Longacre, Doris Janzen. *The RIF (Reduction in Force) Survival Handbook.* Tilden Press.

McCollough, Bonnie. *Bonnie's Household Budget Book*. St. Martin's Press.

Munzert, Alfred W. *Poor Richard's Economic Survival Manual*. Hemisphere.

Ortalada, Robert Jr. *Financial Sanity: How to Live Within Your Means and Still Finance Your Dreams*. Doubleday.

On investing:

Batra, Ravi. *Surviving the Great Depression of 1990*. Simon and Schuster.

Hawken, Paul. *The Next Economy*. Ballantine.

King, John L. *How to Profit from the Next Great Depression*. New American Library.

Meeker-Lowry, Susan. *Economics as if the Earth Really Mattered: A Catalyst Guide to Socially Conscious Investing*. New Society Publishers.

Nichols, Donald. *Investing in Uncertain Times*. Longman Financial Services Publishing.

On career planning:

Petras, Kathryn and Ross. *The Only Job Hunting Guide You'll Ever Need*. Poseidon Press.

Lott, Catherine S. and Arthur C. *How to Land a Better Job*. V.G.M. Career Horizons.

On communication in relationships:

Faber, Adele and Elaine Mazlish. *How to Talk So Kids Will Listen and Listen So Kids Will Talk*. Avon.

Wegscheider-Cruse, Sharon. *Coupleship*. Health Communications.

On meditation and yoga:

Meditation and yoga are best learned from a trained instructor. One international organization that provides individualized instruction free of charge is Ananda Marga. Contact them at the following address to learn of an instructor near you: Ananda Marga, 97-38 42nd Avenue, Corona, New York, NY 11368.

Benson, Herbert. *The Relaxation Response*. Morrow.

Fields, Rick et al. *Chop Wood, Carry Water: A Guide to Finding Spiritual Fulfillment in Everyday Life*. St. Martin's Press.

McClure, Vimala. *Some Still Want the Moon: A Woman's Introduction to Tantra Yoga*. Nucleus Publications.

Prabhavananda, Swami and Christopher Isherwood. *How to Know God: The Yoga Aphorisms of Patanjali*. New American Library.

Ananda Mitra, Acarya. *Yoga for Health*. Ananda Marga Publications.

Meditation Today (An inexpensive periodical). Write to: 68 Wheatley Road, Brookeville, New York, NY 11545.

On stress management:

Charlesworth, Edward and Ronald G. Nathan. *Stress Management*. Athenum.

Davis, Martha et al. *The Relaxation and Stress Reduction Workbook*. New Harbinger Publications.

Eliot, Robert and Dennis L. Breo. *Is it Worth Dying for? How to Make Stress Work for You—Not Against You*. Bantam Books.

Pelletier, Kenneth. *Mind as Healer, Mind as Slayer*. Delta, Seymour Lawrence.

On fitness and health:

Cooper, Kenneth. *The Aerobic Program for Total Well-Being*. Bantam Books.

Cooper, Robert. *Health and Fitness Excellence*. Houghton and Mifflin.

Cousins, Norman. *Anatomy of an Illness* and *The Healing Heart*. W.W. Norton and Company.

Siegel, Bernie. *Love, Medicine, and Miracles*. Harper and Row.

On diet and nutrition:

Ananda Mitra, Acarya. *Food for Thought*. Ananda Marga Publications.

Brody, Jane. *Jane Brody's Nutrition Book*. Bantam Books.

Diamond, Harvey and Marilyn. *Fit for Life*. Warner Books.

Lappe, Francis Moore. *Diet for a Small Planet*. Ballantine.

Null, Gary. *The Vegetarian Handbook*. St. Martin's Press.

Robbins, John. *Diet for a New America*. Stillpoint.

Winick, Myron. *The Columbia Encyclopedia of Nutrition*. Putnam.

On community gardening:

Boston Urban Gardeners. *A Handbook of Community Gardening*. Scribner.

Jobb, Jamie. *The Complete Book of Community Gardening*. William Morrow.

On cooperatives:

Co-op America is a non-profit cooperative association that puts out a regular catalog of goods and services. Contact them at: 2100 M Street, NW, Suite 310, Washington, D.C. 20063.

Honigsberg, Peter Jan, Bernard Kamoroff and Jim Beatty. *We Own It: Starting and Managing Co-ops, Collectives, and Employee Owned Ventures*. Bell Springs Publishing.

Lee, Albert. *How to Save Money Through Group Buying*. Stein and Day.

Wead, Rodney S. *The Neighborhood Coopertive*. General Board of Global Ministries, the United Methodist Church.

Vocations for Social Change. *No Bosses Here*. Alyson Publications.

Wellor, Mary, Janet Hannah, and John Stirling. *Worker Cooperatives in Theory and Practice*. Open University Press.

On barter and labor exchange:

LETS (Labor Exchange Trading System) is an international computerized labor exchange. Contact them at: 375 Johnson Avenue, Courtney, B.C. Canada V9N242.

Gershman, Michael. *Smarter Barter: a Guide to Corporations, Professionals, and Small Businesses*. Viking.

Stapleton, Constance. *Barter: How to Get Almost Anything Without Money*. Scribner.

Simon, Diane Asimow. *The Barter Book*. E.P. Dutton.

ABOUT THE AUTHOR

Mark Friedman currently serves as the editor of *One Magazine* and as the director of the Homeless Families Campaign in Denver, Colorado. He has a bachelor's degree in journalism and a masters degree in management and human relations. For fifteen years he has directed non-profit organizations including arts and human service agencies.

Mark has extensive editing and writing experience and has written numerous articles and the children's book *I Am the Stars*. He is a gifted public speaker and gives lectures and workshops on preparing for the coming depression. He sums up his recommendations for preparing for the depression by advising readers to "make a plan, implement it, and whenever possible, smile."

Index